X95829420

4-13-201)

4n - 20

3

KING OF THE RING

THE HARLEY RACE STORY

Harley Race
with Gerry Tritz

www.SportsPublishingLLC.com

ISBN: 1-58261-818-6

Publishers: Peter L. Bannon and Joseph J. Bannon Sr.
Senior managing editor: Susan M. Moyer
Acquisitions editor: Scott Rauguth
Developmental editor: Dean Miller
Art director: K. Jeffrey Higgerson
Dust jacket design: Joseph Brumleve
Project manager: Kathryn R. Holleman
Imaging: Dustin Hubbart, Heidi Norsen, and Kenneth O'Brien
Photo editor: Erin Linden-Levy
Vice president of sales and marketing: Kevin King
Media and promotions managers: Nick Obradovich (regional), Randy Fouts (national), Maurey Williamson (print)

Printed in the United States of America

Sports Publishing L.L.C.
804 North Neil Street
Champaign, IL 61820

Phone: 1-877-424-2665
Fax: 217-363-2073
Web site: www.SportsPublishingLLC.com

CONTENTS

FOREWORD

Where to start?
There are two words that immediately come to mind when I think of Harley Race.

Respect. Tough.

Quite honestly, I think Harley Race was the toughest pro wrestler of all time—and you can imagine what a huge statement that is for me to make!

At the same time, in all my years in the business, I never met a wrestler who had more respect from the boys than Harley. In fact, he was generally referred to as "The King," and it was a fitting moniker. No man gave more to the business than Harley. He's a champion who would rather show you his scars than his medals.

Much like my father, Harley is a man of great character, a tough man with a strong, hard outside, but once I got to know him I understood that he has a gentle heart and unclouded judgment rarely found in the wrestling business.

I remember a time when Harley worked a world title match for my father's Stampede Wrestling promotion, back in Billings, Montana, in 1978. All the wrestlers got there to find a good crowd on hand, the only problem was that there was no ring! One of my brothers had forgotten to drive the ring truck down! And so, on that night the NWA World Heavyweight Champion wrestled on a mat on the floor of a local high school gym! And he had his usual great match! He did it out of respect for my dad, his fellow wrestlers, and the fans, and I remember my dad commenting to me, "Not too many world champions would have done that!"

There is a pecking order in wrestling. When I first started my career I was quite fortunate that Harley let me ride with him from town to town which, in itself, did a lot to help me earn the respect of the other wrestlers. I listened to Harley's words of advice, and he took care of me in more ways than he'll ever know. As much as I respect him for his incredible skill as a worker, taking some of the greatest bumps ever conceived of, I also respect him for teaching me the art of wrestling and the mechanics behind it.

I had a great career, and I can gratefully acknowledge that without Harley's invaluable advice, Bret "Hitman" Hart wouldn't have been the champion wrestler that I was. Through the loss of Owen and later my father, I'd be remiss not to admit that Harley was a pillar of strength for me to lean on. In the darkest times, I sought out Harley's support and guidance, and he gave me direct and truthful answers, like my dad. Indeed, Harley was like a father to me and a son to my father.

So when Chris Benoit and I were going to lock up in Kansas City to have a classic match in honor of Owen, I felt compelled to call Harley and invite him to be guest ring announcer. His presence punctuated this once-in-a-lifetime moment with the kind of dignity and respect that only a champion's champion commands.

Harley has always been there for me, my dad, the boys, the business—and somehow, through it all, he's managed to stay true to himself.

Harley Race is a legend among legends.

—BRET "HITMAN" HART

TESTIMONY

From the age of 11 to 16, I watched Harley Race on television every Friday night. Today, at the age of 51, I never imagined that I would be writing a paragraph in Harley Race's book, or that 35 years ago, I would ever think that he would be a personal friend of mine today. I can honestly say that Harley Race is one of the nicest, most decent individuals that I have ever had the pleasure of knowing. Harley and B.J. have been a shining star for this community of Eldon, Missouri. The charitable contributions he has made to Eldon and the surrounding areas have been numerous. The business he has generated has been greatly appreciated. I consider it a great honor that Harley calls me a friend. In the ring and out of the ring, Harley has loved life on his terms: honest, decent and with compassion. Congratulations my friend, on all of your accomplishments and success, and especially this book. B.J., we know who the driving force really is.

—ROB FRAZEE
Vice President
Central Bank, Eldon, Missouri

Harley Race is many things to many people. He's a world champion to some and a villain to others. He's handsome, a mad dog, a hero, a "bad guy," a bleach-blond heel, a bleach-blond babyface, and sometimes an archenemy to be regarded with hate and dismay. But to me, he's just "Dad."

Eight-time World Heavyweight Champion Harley Race left big shoes to fill for a kid who grew up in the controversial and confusing – to say the least – world of professional wrestling. His shoes walked past former champions, icons and even kings to prove he was the best the sport had to offer. He paved a path that I could not compete with, only relish. I heard all points of view and manner of questions on what my Dad did for a living. Is it fake? Do they know who will win before the match? Does he really get hurt? What's it like to be Harley Race's son? I took these questions as an indication of one thing: success. Why would they be so interested if they didn't care?

Success is a word given to those who fulfill a lofty objective given by others. Success to me, as taught by my father, is fulfilling what is in your heart. My father has told me more than 1,000 times that he did exactly what he enjoyed for over 40 years, and got paid to do it. His success, he will tell you, lies not in the championships he's won or the honorariums bequeathed upon him, but in the fact that he has led a fulfilling life. "No stone has been left unturned," he will say. "Everything is on the table for the world to see." My father held nothing back, and in being true to that mantra, has nothing left to accomplish. Success has taken him to the top of the world, the bottom, the top, the bottom and the top once again, this time to be judged only by history.

What I have learned in this whirlwind of expectations, media and speculation is that success is in your own eyes. One man's world champion is another man's pigeon. You have to look in the mirror to decide your success. No newspaper, promo or fan can do it for you.

Sometimes shoes are so big that it would be a dishonor to try to fill them. When your father not only redefines a profession, but also advances that profession from an auditorium of 100 to stadiums filled with tens of thousands, that's about as much as one family can do. Harley Race's shoes can't be filled, in my opinion. My eyes will never see that grandeur, only the pride of participation. It is just fine with me to say, "All right, I'll give him that, I'll be the best at something else."

As you enjoy this book, you will find that the success of Harley Race's fulfilled life resides not only in his career, but in his dedication to being a father. From traveling thousands of miles just to see me wrestle one match as a kid, to seeing me off to school every morning that he was at home. Regardless of his post-midnight arrival the night before, my Dad was always there for me, no matter his physical location. His big shoes taught me everything from how to be a man to how to be a father. "A father who is not around as much as he'd like," Dad would say, "has an extra duty to be involved when time permits, even if that means a relationship by telephone." One thing about Harley Race, Dad, was that he never let me down.

This quiet man, who cares much more for others than himself, who is idolized by those that he, himself, looks up to, and who has been known to the family since I can remember as "The Big Teddy Bear" is whom I call Dad. When people confront me with the statement "You're just like your father," I quietly smile to myself and say, "Thank you, God."

—JUSTIN RACE

INTRODUCTION

"The list is endless of guys that were tough guys. But the toughest guy in my estimation that I've ever been in the ring with and as great a competitor as I've ever been in the ring with is Harley Race. He believed who he was, he knew who he was. He had the most self-confidence of anybody I've ever seen, and he lived and breathed our business."
— Ric Flair in *The Ultimate Ric Flair Collection*

Two days before Thanksgiving 1983, the phone rang in my Kansas City home. On the other line was Vince McMahon Jr., the owner of what was quickly becoming the No. 1 wrestling organization in the world. He was also the enemy. "Harley, I'd like to talk to you immediately, face to face. Can I fly you to Connecticut tomorrow?"

I was the World Heavyweight Champion. By all accounts, I should have been on top of the world. Instead, I was down in the dumps, disgusted with wrestling. As far as anyone else knew, I had it all: a seven-year run as champion, money, cars, boats, houses and tens of thousands of fans worldwide. I was practically a household name.

But my championship belt was going to be taken away from me. After that, there wouldn't be the money, the cars, the fans, the fame. And, of all days, it was set to happen on Thanksgiving.

It didn't have to happen this way, Vince told me when I flew to meet him. He wanted me to join the WWF, ending my affiliation with the National Wrestling Alliance before losing the belt to Ric Flair in two days.

McMahon had lured many of the top wrestlers from the NWA, but he didn't have its champion.

I had two choices. I could stay loyal to the NWA, lose the belt, and pray that the WWF didn't run us out of business. Or I could get a fresh start with a new wrestling powerhouse in the twilight of my career, and possibly have a chance to be its champion. Oh, and there was also the $250,000 signing bonus.

It was a decision that would determine the course of the rest of my life ...

For a simple farm boy in rural Missouri, reaching this point in my life was a series of soaring highs and plummeting lows. My life story is one of endless determination and tenacity to be the best at what I do, while always remaining true to myself. My success came at a price, but as you'll learn in this book, that price had nothing to do with selling out or compromising. Like Old Blue Eyes sang, "I did it my way."

ONE

BAD KID MAKES GOOD ON HIS WORD

It was the first week of 10th grade when I found myself in the middle of a knockdown, drag-out brawl during gym class. At least that's the way it would have appeared to an outsider. See, Danny Keever and I were best friends since we were the size of a sack of potatoes. And since then, we wrestled each other pretty much on a daily basis. Now that we had grown to be the two biggest kids in school, it seemed all the more natural. It wasn't uncommon for our classmates to see us rolling around, trying to get the upper hand. So like any other day, we were tangled up during gym class, each trying for a headlock that would give us the advantage. But this day was different—it would alter the course of my life.

What looked brutal to our classmates and teachers was just a healthy, ongoing competition to us. Neither of us knew the first thing about wrestling, but we were driven by a competitive spirit. On this day, it got a little too competitive. In fact, we were downright infuriated with each other. (Danny and I are still friends to this day.) And although we didn't know it at the time, we were drawing the attention of others. I found that out when I felt a knee to the back of my neck, shoving my face firmly into the cold gym floor. Not a calming feeling. My reaction, as you might guess, wasn't calm either. At this moment, I didn't know or care who did it. I shook off the pain, jumped to my feet, spun around and swung. Eldon Steiger, the school's principal and superintendent, hit the floor. And I was on my way out the door.

I was barred from school property until I apologized to the shaken but unhurt principal. I'm not the apologetic type of guy, so it would become a lifetime suspension. I was only 15, but I already knew what I wanted to do with my life. I wouldn't recommend this tactic for anyone else, but getting kicked out of school cleared the way for me to pursue my dream: a career in professional wrestling.

I wasn't born on April 11, 1942, as my altered driver's license would have you believe. (Altering it back was the tough part; more on that later.) It was actually April 11, 1943, and my given name is Harley Leland Race. It's not a stage name, as many people still believe. I was named Harley after one uncle and Leland after another. The name Race can be traced to western England in the 1700s, and to this day there are fewer than 300 Races in the United States.

I was born in Maryville, Missouri, just a few miles away from our home in Quitman. Our family of eight was a big part of the community, if only because it was a community of 139 people. (As of the 2000 Census, the population dropped to 46: 23 males and 23 females.) My parents, Mary and George "Jay" Allen Race, were sharecroppers. To help feed my brother, four sisters and me, Dad also worked as a bus driver. My mother had an even tougher job as a homemaker.

I was happy as a kid, although I often kept to myself. I never seemed to need the social interaction or affirmation that other kids did. It's not that I was antisocial, but I just didn't give a damn whether anyone was around or not. Danny was one of my few close friends, and when we weren't getting each other in headlocks, we were fishing or, on occasion, tipping over outhouses.

I entered professional wrestling about the time in my life when most kids enter amateur wrestling in high school. High school wrestling wasn't an option for me, not just due to the suspension, but because Quitman High School was barely big enough to have teams for the major sports, much less wrestling.

I knew about pro wrestling as a young teenager through radio ads and promotions for wrestling shows that came through the area. Not long after our family plopped down some hard-earned cash for a new black-and-white television set, I saw my first match on TV. It was the second semester of my freshman year of high school, just months before my suspension. Cable didn't exist then, so we picked from three channels. KQTV Channel 2 out of St. Joseph was the clearest, and it televised wrestling.

Sonny Myers had a stellar wrestling career. His accolades included being the 14-time NWA Central States Heavyweight Champion. After retiring, he was a referee before being elected sheriff in Buchanan County, Missouri.[1]

I'm not certain who the wrestlers were during that first match I saw on TV, but I'm fairly certain Myers was one of them. I just remembered that I was in awe, and I told my family right then and there: "That's what I'm going to do."

Of course, they all had a good laugh at my expense. Actually, I think my announcement impressed my sisters: Nadine, twins Carolyn and Marilyn, and the youngest, Linda. They were the only members of the family naïve enough to think I could make good on my word. Mom politely discouraged me, while Dad was a little less diplomatic. He may have said something about me having a "snowball's chance in hell" of ever wrestling professionally. As for my brother, Tom, he couldn't stop laughing long enough to talk to me about it.

About the time I was kicked out of school, my family moved to Clarinda, Iowa. It's a small southwest Iowa town most notable for being the birthplace of swing-era big band leader Glenn Miller. My folks moved there to take jobs at a mental health facility. I stayed behind to run the farm. We had livestock on about 15 acres around the house, and we grew vegetables on adjacent land that we leased from other farmers.

For the first time in my life, I was on my own. I worked on our farm and earned some cash by helping out at another near-

by farm. I spent what little I had wisely, buying food before anything else. My grocery list mostly consisted of huge containers of
macaroni, tomato sauce and a five-pound bag of sugar. Call it
poor man's pasta, but it suited me just fine. And I ate it pretty
much every day of the week. Another staple of my diet then was
potted meat, which was convenient because you didn't have to
refrigerate it until after you opened it.

I was only 15, but I was holding my own on the farm. Not
that there weren't glitches. One morning when I went to refill
the wood stove, only a few embers of wood remained from the
previous night. So I added wood and paper, and then doused it
in kerosene to get it started. By the time I found a match to
throw onto it, the air was thick with kerosene fumes. The match
ignited the kerosene and the fumes, sending a blast of fire directly into my face. I knew right away that I had burned myself pretty good. I also knew that running around in circles screaming
wouldn't do any good. At best, a few cattle might have heard. So
I walked about 12 blocks into downtown Quitman and found
someone who would take me to the Maryville hospital 10 miles
down the road. My face was toasted, and a good portion of my
hair was gone. For the next five weeks, the bandages around my
head made me look like the Invisible Man.

Running the farm had its ups and downs, but I never lost
sight of my goal. My first step into the world of professional
wrestling was an unlikely one: I got a job at another farm, this
one 30 miles away in Savannah, Missouri. Truthfully, it was the
best career move I could have made. The farm was owned by the
Zbyszko family, and they weren't just farmers. Stanislaus Zbyszko
(real name: Stan Cyganiewicz) was an old man by then, just a few
years from his death. But in his prime, he was a champion
wrestler. He came to the United States in 1909 and quickly
found wrestling success. He won more than 1,000 matches
before losing a controversial match to Frank Gotch, the best pro
wrestler of the day and one of the all-time greats. Zbyszko lost
most of his wealth in World War I and then returned to the
United States to defeat Ed "The Strangler" Lewis for the World

Heavyweight Title in 1921.[2] Zbyszko's brother, Wladek, was probably 10 or 15 years younger, and a fine wrestler, despite never owning a championship belt.

On their farm, I planted and tilled crops, and I planted hay and hauled it from the field to the barn. In the evenings, I badgered them into teaching me wrestling. It was part of the deal, but I still had to badger them. Mostly what they taught me were submission holds. They'd put me in one, and say: "Try to get out." The more I tried, the more I wore myself out or hurt myself. The sight of me hobbling around their farm for days on end wasn't uncommon.

By this time, my parents still thought a career in wrestling was a pipe dream, but they were resigned to the fact that I was going to try. That fall, I made the 42-mile trip to St. Joseph to introduce myself to a man named Gust Karras. (Although Gust was his official name, he went by Gus.) I had heard about his carnival wrestling shows on the radio. Gus was a successful carnival owner, a shrewd businessman, and an all-around nice guy. We would later become business partners.

Gus saw that I had the size to be a wrestler, so he sent a couple of his wrestlers and me to the YMCA to see if I had any potential. They reported back to Gus that, short of breaking one of my limbs, they couldn't get me to submit. Gus figured that with that kind of stupidity to risk my own safety, I'd be a perfect fit for his carnival wrestling.

Carnival patrons paid extra to get into the wrestling tent. On hot summer nights, you could add humidity and 20 degrees to get the feel for what it was like inside the tent. Combine that with cigarette smoke and 200 rowdy men, and you start to get the idea of the atmosphere. The origins of professional wrestling can be traced to carnivals in the 1800s. And like those early days of professional wrestling, there was a gimmick involved to bring in the money and keep a relative degree of safety for the wrestlers.

Gus explained to me how it worked: One of his wrestlers would enter the ring and challenge the townspeople to wrestle him, offering cash to anyone tough enough to whip him. While the traveling tough guy stirred up the crowd with his boasts and insults, the townspeople would look around for one of their own to step forward. What they didn't know is that a second wrestler for Gus was playing the part of one of the locals. The incognito wrestler would begin by telling the people standing next to him: "Who's he to talk down to us like that? I oughta teach that guy a lesson myself." Soon enough, members of the crowd would volunteer their new "local" hero, who eventually would be "talked into" going toe to toe with the challenger.

Because I was young and didn't have the telltale look of a grizzled carnie veteran, I usually played the part of the local. Often I would lose the match. That way, through word of mouth, the tough-guy reputation of the carnival wrestler would be boosted when he traveled to the next city. But if the cocky carnival wrestler did his job of inciting the audience too well, (i.e, if he drew too much "heel heat") then it was in our best interest to have him lose to me. Otherwise, we ran the risk of a drunken lynch mob forming against the tough-guy carnival wrestler.

They were classic heel vs. babyface match-ups, and the audience ate it up. It provided an entertaining show, while furthering the illusion that they were witnessing a true brawl. The "heel" didn't have to forfeit the operation's money if he lost, since the "babyface" also was a carnival employee. And it was much safer than really allowing townspeople to get in the ring.

But it didn't always work that way. Sometimes a local tough guy would jump into the ring before the plant in the audience had a chance. That's when things became interesting—and more dangerous. Either way, it was a style of wrestling known as "catch as catch can," meaning submission wrestling. When we wrestled each other, we watched out for each other in the ring, just like pro wrestlers continue to do today. But wrestling a local was more dangerous, usually to him. If you got hold of a finger, and the guy didn't give up, you broke the finger. In this pre-lawsuit crazy era, arms and legs were fair game, too. We generally tried to avoid injuries in the ring when possible, but it didn't always work that way.

On many occasions, I was the challenger, and I often wound up facing some legitimately tough old farmers who knew it was their chance of a lifetime to prove their mettle in public against a real wrestler—or as close to one as you can be at the age of 16. There were times some of those mean old bastards had me on the ropes for real. I knew if I lost the match, the farmer would get paid and I wouldn't. But if I got disqualified, I got paid and he didn't. So I quickly learned to throw my head into their noses if it looked like they were getting the upper hand. A well-placed head-butt preserved my pay many days.

I wasn't just wrestling for pride like these guys I was facing—this was my living. And you don't screw with a man's ability to earn a living. Even at the age of 16, I knew that much.

[1] Information about Sonny Myers taken from www.geocities.com/percivalafriend/friend052603.htm and www.100megsfree4.com/wiawrestling/pages/nwa/nwacsh.htm

[2] Information about Stanislaus Zbyszko taken from www.wrestlingmuseum.com

TWO

LONE STAR

"For Harley, the guns went along with the fast driving. If you pushed the clock back 100 years, he would have been a sheriff or marshal in the Old West. He could have been a gunslinger."

—Nick Bockwinkle

Growing up, I wasn't the kind of guy who looked for trouble, but it always seemed to be heading my way. And when it did, I didn't back down. Northwest Missouri was a rough place in the early '60s. Gangs existed in many places across the United States at the time, including northwest Missouri. In our neck of the woods, it wasn't the Crips and Bloods or Hell's Angels, just a loosely formed band of juvenile delinquents. One thing separated us from most areas: In addition to a boys' gang, we also had a girls' gang. And, like the boys, these young ladies had a taste for violence.

The boys' gang sometimes set up their own unofficial toll stop at a bridge on Highway 59 between Fairfax and Tarkio. They would charge maybe eight to 10 cars to get on the bridge, then split before the cops got there. The girls' gang was ruthless. It once castrated a boy, who later committed suicide.

I was no model citizen, but I never wanted to be associated with any such groups. To send this message loud and clear, I strung together seven needles, dipped them into Indian ink, and sank the needles into my forearm. I spelled out the word "Lone Star" and drew a star underneath the words. It was my first tattoo.

My only confrontation with the boys' gang happened when a group of them decided to hassle me one day while my car was parked near them. What they didn't realize is that I had a shotgun in the back seat of my car, and I wasn't afraid to use it. The shotgun belonged to my dad, who had fired it one day without knowing that hornets had built a nest inside the barrel. The shot split the barrel, and so Dad sawed off the split end to salvage the gun. Anyway, the gang members didn't look so tough when I pulled out a sawed-off shotgun. When I squeezed the trigger, pellets sprayed the grill of their car, and steam and engine fluids shot into the air. They never bothered me again.

You'd think that seeing my Dad have a shotgun practically blow up in his face would turn me off from guns, but it actually had the opposite effect. I started collecting them. I was especially fascinated with one-of-a-kind models, such as the 1917 German Luger, one of my first purchases. It had a spring-loaded case and was fully automatic. It wasn't much for accuracy, but it sprayed bullets quick enough that you were bound to hit your target soon enough. It was basically an early version of the tommy guns popularized by Chicago gangsters in the 1920s. I once took my Luger and pointed it at a small tree that was several inches thick at the bottom. I held down the trigger and peppered the tree trunk with enough lead to cut through it like a chain saw.

By the late 1960s, I owned literally hundreds of guns of all makes and models, and, by then, I carried one with me at all times. More on that later, but I'll jump ahead a few years to tell you one gun-related story now.

While I was wrestling in Minneapolis in the late 1960s, Johnny Valentine decided to play a prank on another wrestler, Jay York, who wrestled as "The Alaskan." Valentine had somehow managed to put lighter fluid in York's asthma spray. Like other nights after he wrestled, York put the spray up to his mouth and gave himself a blast of it in the locker room. As you could imagine, he started gagging on the lighter fluid, and wasn't too pleased when he got his breath back.

Not long after that, I was in a dressing room with those two and a couple other wrestlers, Larry Hennig and John Powers. York apparently thought Valentine swapped his spray with lighter fluid again. He pulled out a handgun, pointed it at Valentine and said: "I told you that if you ever jacked with my asthma spray again, I'm gonna kill you."

He pulled the trigger, and the blast sent Valentine into a shower stall on his back. Then he turned to us and said, "I can't have any witnesses to this." He pointed it first at Powers, who basically begged for his life. Then he trained the pistol's barrel on Hennig. Valentine, meanwhile, was twitching on the floor. By the time York started to point his gun at me, he realized that he was staring down the barrel of my gun. By then the room had filled with other wrestlers who heard the first shot and ran into the room.

"Either you lower that gun, or you're going to be right there next to Valentine," I said.

"Harley, wait, this is just a joke," York pleaded. "Valentine, get up!"

It turns out York fired a blank at Valentine after the two had conspired to scare the daylights out of us in their elaborate prank. Of course, I didn't know that at the time, and I wasn't about to take chances. Their hoax backfired, and it damn near cost York his life.

The vast majority of my confrontations, however, were settled the old-fashioned way. Not long after I started working for Gus,

a punk a few years older than me from nearby Skidmore started
to become infamous in northwest Missouri. Ken Rex McElroy
came from a nice family, and he seemed like a decent enough
kid. But before adulthood, a mean streak took hold of him.

Kenny started out stealing grain and livestock. He reportedly
fathered dozens of children by different women. But he was best
known as the "Skidmore bully" for threatening, intimidating and
roughing up anyone in his path. At his most extreme, Kenny shot
a local grocer in the neck after a dispute over Kenny's kid stealing from the store. Kenny had never been convicted of anything
previously, because, as townspeople said, he was good at intimidating his victims. But the grocer, Bo Bowenkamp, survived the
shotgun blast, and pressed charges. Kenny was found guilty of
second-degree assault, but remained free on bond pending an
appeal during the summer of 1981.

The townspeople had had enough. On July 10, 1981, about
60 men met with the sheriff to decide how to deal with Kenny.
After the sheriff left, someone walked into the meeting and
spread the word that Kenny had entered D&G's Tavern in
Skidmore. Many of the men headed there and entered the tavern. After finishing his beer, Kenny left the bar and entered his
truck. The men followed him out, watching Kenny start his truck
and light a cigarette. Kenny's third wife, Trena, shouted that she
saw a man with a rifle. Then, 10 shots rang out from behind. He
was hit in the neck and twice in the head. Between a dozen and
60 people witnessed the execution, but none cooperated with
authorities. More than two decades later, the case remains open
but unsolved. The story made national news, including a segment
on "60 Minutes," and has been the subject of a book and a TV
movie called *In Broad Daylight*.[1]

My run-in with Kenny happened about 20 years before he
was killed—just about the time he was starting to gain a reputation for terrorizing townspeople. Each month, some of the area's
retirees would go for a beer after receiving their pension checks.
Kenny knew which day of the month he could find them in the
bars, and he was notorious for bullying them out of their money.

I happened to be in a bar one evening when Kenny started pulling that crap, and I wasn't about to let it continue. So I walked up to him and said, "Not today, Kenny. Today it's you and me." I landed a solid left hook to his face, and he struggled to get back on his feet. When he did, he promptly left the bar. Everyone in the bar thanked me, but it took a vigilante mob two decades later to end his reign of terror against the community.

To a certain extent, I was a product of my environment, as stories like the one above demonstrate. But the older I get, the more my family and friends see another side of Harley Race. Even as a kid, I had feelings and emotions like anyone else. I tried to be polite and considerate. And I knew that no matter how tough I was, it didn't matter if I didn't have God in my life.

If that didn't surprise you, this might: It was about this time in my life that I studied to be a Methodist minister.

Actually, it was right around the time I started wrestling. I was raised as a Nazarene, but a Free Methodist minister talked me into going to his church. I've since forgotten the man's name, but he was a kind man who became a positive influence in my life. He introduced me to his wife and family, and they, in turn, treated me like family. He told me that attending church wasn't enough—I needed to turn my life over to Christ. I started meeting with him and another young man, and we would read the Bible together and discuss its meaning. Once, I attended a revival with him. Through a six-month period, I progressed from studying the Bible to studying to become a Free Methodist minister. When I had carnival matches, he often would show up to support me.

But the wrestling bug had bit me hard, and because of time constraints, I phased out my minister training. I've since changed my faith to Lutheran. Obviously, I can't say I've always lived my life according to the Gospel, but I can say I've never lost my faith in God. These days, more than ever, I realize the importance of keeping Him in my life.

My career in professional wrestling was under way, even if I was just a glorified carnie worker at this point. Like the other carnies, I arrived before the shows to set up the wrestling tent. I was also among the last wrestlers who learned the "carnie" language, and I can speak it to this day.

The language is a form of pig Latin that is heavy on the z's. Carnival workers developed it in the 1800s as a way for them to privately communicate with one another when speaking in front of carnival patrons. It was needed because, like today, many of the games of skill at carnivals are rigged. In order to separate patrons (they're called "marks" in the business) from their money, they sometimes needed to communicate without the patrons knowing what was being said. In wrestling, carnie was used for a similar purpose. It allowed us to choreograph moves in the ring without anyone knowing.

Gus not only gave me my first break, but he continued to help me by occasionally sending seasoned wrestlers to train me. During and after my carnival period, I also got sporadic but valuable training from talents such as Ray Gordon, Bobby Graham and "Killer" Buddy Austin.

It didn't take long to figure out that wrestling—even carnival wrestling—paid well. Gus would give me $10-$12 a match, and I'd often wrestle up to five matches a night. It was that or work on the farm for about $1 an hour. But the carnival season was ending, and my career was just beginning. Working carnivals got my foot in the door, and Gus was willing to give me a shot at professional wrestling outside carnivals.

My first match was against a man by the name of Bill Cole in Waterloo, Iowa, in the spring of 1960. Not only did I get my ass thoroughly kicked in the ring, but I got it chewed afterward in the dressing room. "You rushed everything, and you were way too aggressive," other wrestlers told me. "Let things happen naturally," they said. "If you're wrestling for 20 minutes, don't blow yourself out in the first 10 minutes."

They were right. I wanted so badly to put on a good show for my maiden bout that I was running around the ring like some crazy kid jacked up on too much Mountain Dew. I suspect that Cole, who had experience as an amateur wrestler, put up with my amateur antics for only as long as necessary to get his pay-check.

I learned from my mistakes. Soon I became better at pacing myself and looking more natural in the ring. Other wrestlers helped with constructive criticism: "Don't slam your opponent on the ground, then pick him back up all in the same motion," they told me. "Otherwise, the audience is left wondering why the hell you slammed him in the first place." I was soaking up their advice and trying to apply it in the ring each night. Within six months, I was probably wrestling at the level of many wrestlers with two years' experience.

It was with the carnival that I first started using what would become a signature move later in my career: the head-butt. I learned early on in my wrestling career that I had a hard head, and I started using it to my advantage. I won many of my carnival matches with a firm head-butt. Sometimes my opponent wouldn't know what hit him. He would tap out, not knowing whether the head-butt was intentional or by accident. I cut open many people's eyebrows with the move, and I imagine I broke a few noses.

---

[1] Background information on the McElroy case was taken from an Associated Press article by Scott Charton that was published in July 2001.

THREE

"CAREER-ENDING" TRAGEDY

"I had an advantage over a lot of wrestlers; I was a second-generation wrestler. Harley didn't have that advantage. Believe me, it was great, because everybody knew my father, all the promoters around the country. It's very different to make it on your own. Harley truly did come up through the school of hard knocks. And he became a great performer, too. He was very much a natural: natural ability, and a pretty doggone tough guy, too, which you had to be in this business."

—Terry Funk

My first traveling partner was a man who, even on a diet, would keep Andre the Giant suspended in air during a seesawing contest. William Cobb was a novelty act who weighed in at around 700 pounds for most of his wrestling career, but, at one point, topped 1,000 pounds. He went by the name Happy Humphrey.

Humphrey started professional wrestling in 1953, after wrestling a bear for 28 minutes.[1] I met Humphrey in 1960 in St. Joseph, Missouri, through Gus. My job was to drive him from one territory to another. The job paid five dollars a day, plus room and board. During that period, we also wrestled each other regularly, and I earned another $25 each time I wrestled. I also started refereeing matches, earning the same per match.

Humphrey drew good-sized crowds. Everyone wanted to see this enormous grappler who rarely lost. To me, he had made the big-time, and I was glad to latch on for the ride. Besides, he was a kind-hearted man, and I got along great with him.

I wrestled Humphrey more times than I would like to remember. What can you do with a 700-plus pound man in the ring? Well, since Humphrey trusted me, he would let me do some things that he wouldn't let other wrestlers do—things like a headlock takedown. Much of what I did in the ring was designed to make him look like a Superman. I'd get him in a wristlock, and he'd straighten out his arm, sending me tumbling across the ring. It was then that I started learning to really "sell the bumps"—in other words, exaggerate the reaction from being hit. Many times, acting like it hurt wasn't necessary. It did hurt. Sometimes, I would begin to wrestle Humphrey when the territory's big heel would jump in the ring and say, "Wait a minute! I want to wrestle him. You can't beat him." The match typically would end when the heel got disqualified for doing something outrageous to Humphrey.

I drove Humphrey in a 1951 Pontiac that was custom made to fit him. The doors opened from the front to the back, and the shock absorbers were re-enforced. I never witnessed it, but I heard about promoters weighing Humphrey on scales at meat factories, since ordinary scales were no match for his extraordinary girth. What I did witness was even more gruesome—Humphrey in his birthday suit. Because he was so huge, many ordinary showers didn't accommodate him too well. But because I had to sit next to him in the car, I quickly learned that we needed to find a way to bathe him regularly. What I ended up doing—and I did this more than once—is to have him lay on the ground with his clothes off while I squeezed liquid soap on his body. I then used a mop to scrub him and a garden hose to wash him off. I hope not too many bystanders witnessed this strange bathing ritual—I can only imagine what would have gone through their heads.

Because of his size, Humphrey was tough to wrestle. But he was one of the nicest men I've ever known—just a big, jovial guy. He loved kids, especially his young fans. He was one of the few wrestlers of that era who would spend time socializing with his fans, signing every last autograph. The only thing he didn't like is when overzealous fans questioned him about his weight.

Humphrey's oversized body was caused by a pituitary gland disorder. Before I met him, he had surgery to cut about 100 pounds of fat from his body, but he regained the weight. In 1962, after my tour with Humphrey had finished, he was confined to a bed and sought help from a Georgia medical school. He became a test subject and lost 630 pounds through a strict diet. He quit wrestling and lived until 1989.

When I had matches close to home, Mom and Dad would come to watch. By this time, Dad was no longer laughing at my desire to be a wrestler. He had done a 180-degree shift and had become my No. 1 fan.

Unfortunately, that caused problems a couple different times.

During a match in St. Joseph, once right before I met Humphrey, I was lying on my back with my opponent pummeling me from above. Out of the corner of my eye, I could see a panicked look on the referee's face as he looked toward ringside, then back toward me.

"Your dad's trying to get in the ring," he whispered.

By this time, Dad was getting into the ring. Dad was a pretty small guy, standing only five feet, eight inches tall. But he was determined to save me from the very serious injuries I was apparently about to sustain.

The security staff was just catching up to him. So I rolled over, got up and grabbed Dad before the security guards could rough him up. I quickly helped him out of the ring and said: "I can't be watching you and doing what I'm doing, Dad. I know what I'm doing. Let me do it."

What made matters worse was that this was the second time it had happened. So after the match, we sat down for a father-son talk. Only this time, it was me doing the talking.

"This can't happen again, Dad. Either you're going to have to control yourself or you can't come to any more of my matches."

Dad was absolutely convinced that my opponents and I were trying to beat each other's brains out in the ring, and he was afraid for his son's life. I told him I could take care of myself. What I didn't tell him was that my opponents were really my teammates and that we were working together to entertain the crowds. This was back in an era when it was so taboo to smarten anyone up to the business that I didn't tell anyone. Not even my own parents.

In a way, my dad's concern for my safety was a compliment—it meant that our performance was convincing to at least one person in the building.

By 1961, I was making a living from professional wrestling and enjoying every minute of it. Humphrey and I had been wrestling and traveling together for nearly a year. We were based in Nashville, but I often returned to northwest Missouri to visit a girl who I had fallen in love with. Everything was going right, but I had no idea how quickly my life would soon be torn apart.

Vivian Jones and I didn't attend school together, but we had known each other since our early teens. She was a very attractive girl who was about five years my senior. Her family lived in Guilford, Missouri, about a half-hour away from St. Joseph. She married a man—also an acquaintance of mine—from Maryville. One day, while Vivian was pregnant with Tonya, the second of her two children, her husband was killed in a senseless bar fight. Vivian and I started dating less than a year after his death, and we were married a couple years later in Cleveland on November 26, 1961.

On Christmas night, we were driving from my parents' house in Clarinda, Iowa, to her parents' house in Guilford. It recently had snowed about 17 inches, and the road we were driving on had just reopened earlier that day. At about 12:15 a.m. on December 26, our car and a tractor-trailer loaded full of eggs were approaching each other while driving along Highway 71 between Maryville and Wilcox. Neither of us saw the other vehicle approaching because we were both climbing the hill from different sides, and there was a snowdrift near the top. The truck driver swerved into my lane to avoid the snowdrift, then swerved again in a last-ditch effort to avoid us. The tractor-trailer jack-knifed, and both the cab and the trailer slammed into us head-on, sending our car reeling 80 feet.

Both Vivian and I were pronounced dead at the scene. My pulse was undetectable. Only after I moved slightly in the ambulance on the way into town did they realize I was still alive.

I regained consciousness in the Maryville hospital a few days later. When I asked where my wife was, the doctor in the room said: "What wife? You don't have one." I know the son of a bitch only said it through ignorance, but he's lucky I was in no condition to get out of the hospital bed. If I had been, I wouldn't have had a doctor, either.

She was buried that same day. I wasn't told that at the time, because I was still fighting for my own life. Later I was told that she was killed instantly. We had been married one month to the day, and we were expecting our first child.

At the same time I was grieving, I was also learning the extent of my own injuries. The most damage was done to my right leg, and the doctors were preparing to amputate it.

About that time, Gus had driven to see my parents. When he heard they likely would need to amputate my leg, he went to the hospital and convinced the doctors to have me sent to a St. Joseph bone specialist for a second opinion. "They can cut the leg off down there as easily as they can here. Let's try to save it," he told the doctors in Maryville. They agreed, and took me to Dr. Jobe Kaloski, who operated on my leg on January 1 in an attempt to save it. The operation was a success. On January 7, he repaired damage to my arm and then removed steel and glass fragments from my skull three days after that.

But I didn't come out of the wreck unscathed, emotionally or physically. Two metal braces and 12 pins were inserted to hold my shattered forearm together. My right knee needed four metal screws.

I was later awarded $35,000 from the accident, payable when I turned 21. But by that time, the two lawyers managing the money somehow only had $10,000 left. I was never given an explanation of the missing money. The lawyers were friends of Gus Karras, so I didn't consider suing them.

Soon after the wreck, Dr. Kaloski stood over me at my bedside and firmly told me that I'd probably never walk again, and that my wrestling career was definitely over. But even back then, I had a stubborn sense of determination, and I immediately took it as a challenge. "I'll send you ringside tickets to my first match," I told him.

My recovery took 21 long months. At first, I stayed with my parents in Clarinda while recovering. I wore braces on my legs for 18 months, then spent another three months recuperating.

To this day, the accident and my rehabilitation are parts of my life that are painful to think about. I've long since repressed many of the details. I just know I tried to concentrate on my rehabilitation so I wouldn't dwell on the loss of my wife. Plus, I was determined to prove my doctor wrong and return to wrestling. Although it was early in my career, pro wrestling was still a dream come true, and I wasn't about to give it up easily.

My first return to the wrestling ring was a match in northwest Missouri in late 1962. Like I promised, I sent Dr. Kaloski ringside tickets, and he showed up to cheer me on.

At school, I had a friend by the name of Danny Carr. Several years after my accident, his brother David went to fight in Vietnam. After his tour of duty, he returned to northwest Missouri, got married and had a child. But then he made the mistake of returning for another tour, and he didn't make it home alive.

In the mid-'60s, I received my draft paperwork just like all the other guys my age. But when I reported for my physical, they took one look at my leg and sent me home. If I had been called on to fight for my country, I would have. But I can't say that I was ever gung-ho about going to Vietnam. I didn't agree with a lot of things about the war. The more it dragged on, the more I thought that if we're going to go to war like that, we should have a plan for a quick and decisive victory. But it seemed like every day, more and more kids around my age weren't coming back alive. When I found out David died there, the first thing that ran through my mind is that—if not for an act of God—it could have easily have been me. So if there was any good that came out of the wreck, it was that it kept me out of Vietnam.

Thankfully, my problems at the time were far less significant than dodging bullets in a foreign country. One of the biggest issues I was trying to resolve was to untangle myself from the web of deceit I created when I forged my driver's license. I turned 21 in 1964, and I no longer needed a fake ID either for driving or for drinking. So I wanted to set the record straight: I was born in 1943, not 1942.

The problem was that, first, I had to admit that not only did I essentially lie about my age for years, but I had committed a crime. I had taken my driver's license to school and used a typewriter to change the "3" to a "2."

My parents and I talked to various county and state officials. At first they had a hard time believing that all their records were wrong. Then, when they did believe me, they threatened me with criminal charges for forging my age in the first place. Finally, my parents were able to get records of my birth from the Maryville hospital to prove my age, and they made the change. But the entire process took more than a year to correct. Since I was out on the road, my parents took on the job of wading through the bureaucracy needed to make the change. By the time it was done, they were aggravated as hell at me, and right-fully so.

[1] Some background information on Happy Humphrey was used from Slam! Sports at http://slam.canoe.ca/slam/wrestling/home.html

FOUR

THE EARLY YEARS

"He came up and wrestled (in Minneapolis) and we started talking and soon we clicked. I was the strength and he was the agility. We convinced promoters we had a good combination of talent to offer. They put us together, and it was a magical deal."

—Larry Hennig

In 1963, I reunited with Humphrey in Nashville, and we hit the road with the same intensity as before my wreck. In the year we had traveled together, we logged 100,000 miles on that poor Pontiac. We wrestled in the states of Missouri, Kentucky, Alabama, Arkansas and Louisiana.

After about six months, I met a kid in Nashville named Billy Strong, who wrestled under the name John Long. We looked a lot alike, and he was looking for a tag-team partner. So I soon became his "brother," Jack Long. It was this partnership that gave me my first belt when we won the Southern Tag Team Championship. A few months later, I won my first singles title:

The Southwestern Heavyweight Championship. It was a big deal at the time. For the first time in my career, I had recognition beyond people just patting me on the back and saying "good job."

It probably also gave me a more cocky attitude. Around this time, I was challenging fans to get in the ring with me. When they were stupid enough to do it, I figured that gave me the legal green light to teach them a lesson. I would motion to the security staff to let them through, then put them in a submission move that would leave them squealing in front of the audience. If they were tough-looking guys who were bigger than me, I didn't take any chances. I would surprise them with head-butts—sometimes breaking their noses—before they knew what happened. Not a lot of fans climbed into the ring with me. The few who did were usually years older than me. And none of them ever beat me.

Not long after we became partners, my dad asked me why he never saw me in any wrestling magazines. I pulled one out and showed him where they had written about Jack Long. "That's me," I said.

"You've already got a unique name," he replied. "Why would you wrestle as anyone else?" So after John and I parted ways, I went back to Harley Race. I only wrestled under aliases two other nights that I can recall. Once, at the request of a promoter, I wrestled in Chicago as The Great Mortimer in 1963. Another time, I had to hide my identity to wrestle as a favor for an old friend. You'll get the scoop on that match later in the book.

During my tag-team partnership with John Long, we wrestled throughout Tennessee. After wrestling at the old Memphis Auditorium, we'd often return backstage to find Memphis's No. 1 wrestling fan waiting for us: Elvis Presley. Elvis loved to chat with us and the other wrestlers after our matches, and he often used former wrestlers as his bodyguards. I knew Elvis when he was the king of rock 'n' roll. It's too bad he didn't live long enough to see me take on the title of "King." I think he would have been proud.

John and I wrestled around the Nashville area for about six months when another setback occurred. We were wrestling in Glasgow, Kentucky, one night when I decided to show off an aerial maneuver that I recently learned: a backflip from the top rope in which I land on my feet. I landed right where a wrestler from the previous match had spit in the ring. My right leg slipped on the spit as my leg was absorbing the shock of landing. It twisted sideways and snapped my fibula near the ankle.

I finished the match, then made the 100-mile drive back to Nashville before seeking medical treatment. I returned to Missouri and stayed there until my leg healed. When I started back, I wrestled in my home state for awhile before heading to Amarillo, Texas, for about five months. It was during that time that I met one of the all-time great wrestling families: the Funks.

Dory Funk Sr. started wrestling a decade before I did. Funk's oldest son, Dory Jr., was just starting his own wrestling career, and his youngest son, Terry, had recently started college. Dory Sr. was a respected scientific wrestler and a former champion. Both of his sons would take after him.

When I first met Dory Sr., he was running what was known as the "Amarillo territory." Texas was divided into three chunks that were parts of the more than two dozen NWA territories across the United States. The Amarillo territory also included part of New Mexico, running from Albuquerque down to El Paso, Texas, then east to Abilene and north to include the whole Texas panhandle. They sometimes ran shows in the panhandle area of Oklahoma.

I was wrestling for Dory Sr. near Lovington, Texas, on the night of November 22, 1963. President Kennedy had been shot and killed earlier that day in Dallas, and I pleaded unsuccessfully with Dory to cancel the event. If for no other reason than no one was going to show up, I said. "Not only was the president killed here in our own state, but he was a Catholic," I said. "The state has tons of Hispanics, and they're all Catholic. Christ wrestling the devil won't draw a crowd tonight." Like I suspected, the crowd was tiny. But we went on with the show.

By this time, I had remarried, and my second wife, Sandra Jones, was traveling with me to San Francisco. We were just pulling into Albuquerque, New Mexico, when a tingling sensation in my legs gave me a quick warning of what was about to come. Before I could react, my legs went numb. My wife pulled my foot off the gas pedal and slid the stick shift into neutral. We were able to stop the car and trade places before I wrecked the car, but it was a close call.

A day earlier, I had wrestled in Amarillo and had taken a good bump that sent me over the top ropes, falling on my back on the edge of the ring. It wasn't the first time I had been hurt, but after my legs went numb, it was the first time I realized how dangerous my chosen profession could be. Luckily, by the time we got to San Francisco, the feeling had returned to my legs. But it was only the beginning of what would become a lifetime of back problems.

I hated California and couldn't wait to get the hell out. Regardless of where I was driving in California, the drive seemed to take at least two hours of my life that I would never get back. If I got to a match early, then I sat around for another couple hours. But if I didn't leave early enough, I'd risk getting stuck in traffic and missing my match. Then I'd waste an equal amount of time returning. I'd pull in just in time to get a little sleep and do it all over again the next day.

I returned to the Kansas City area after three months, but there was no welcoming committee from the wrestling world there to greet me. The area had more wrestlers than events to employ them, so I wasn't wrestling nearly every night like I did in California. To supplement my income, I bought a hay truck and hauled hay from farmers' fields to their barns. It was the start of the growing season, so it was a good opportunity to make money. I charged 10 cents per bale and often baled 1,000 a day. After paying the two kids who helped me each day, I could come home with $70. On nights that I had wrestling matches, my older brother would take over driving the truck.

One Monday night I drove to Omaha, Nebraska, to wrestle a match taped in an Omaha television studio. I wrestled a man by the name of Verne Gagne.

Gagne was a standout amateur wrestler at the University of Minnesota, winning titles in 1948 and 1949. He reached great heights as a professional wrestler, too, as an eight-time titleholder in the American Wrestling Association, an organization that he owned. In 1999, *Sports Illustrated* put him at No. 24 on a list of top 50 Minnesota sports figures.

After wrestling Gagne, he said to me, "I have the perfect tag-team partner for you. His name is Larry Hennig." Hennig was a champion wrestler at Robbinsdale High School in Minnesota. He first took notice of Hennig after watching the 1954 Minnesota state wrestling championships and seeing a young Hennig win the championship for his weight division. Hennig was also an all-America football player who won a scholarship to play at the University of Minnesota. But after a year in college, Hennig was married with a child on the way. He needed a way to support his family, so he quit college and learned the pro wrestling ropes from Gagne. Between his amateur training and the solid technical training he learned from Gagne, Hennig was starting to see success after a couple years on the pro side. He was headlining matches and even had a stint as AWA tag-team champion with Duke Hoffman as his partner.

I had met Hennig previously when we were both wrestling in Amarillo, and I jumped at the opportunity to work with him. Our partnership lasted throughout the second half of the '60s, and our friendship would last a lifetime. Our years together would give us both our first taste of national fame and wealth.

It didn't take long for our partnership to click. We wrestled together the same day we agreed to become partners. Soon, we were being promoted around Minneapolis as "Handsome" Harley Race and "Pretty Boy" Larry Hennig. We were cocky and showed a reckless disregard for rules, officials or anything else that stood between us and the tag-team championship.

We wasted no time gunning for the top dogs: Dick the Bruiser and The Crusher. They were two peas in a pod: beer-guzzling, barrel-chested tough guys who each weighed 260 pounds, chomped cigars and liked to talk trash. They were also two of the most feared and hated heels in wrestling.

The Bruiser was a former NFL player named Richard Afflis who became the blue-collar crowd's antihero. He boasted about "bustin' brains" of his opponents with a voice that was gravelly from a crushed esophagus during his football days. A cartoon character's face couldn't contort in anger better than his.

Reggie "The Crusher" Lisowski's sandy blond hair was about the only discernable difference between him and Bruiser, who wore his hair in a crew cut. And like Bruiser, he might as well have got his technical wrestling degree from a Cracker Jack box. They were brawlers to the core.[1] Crusher could take his lickings better than a Timex. He didn't just tolerate pain, he basked in it. And the more his blood spilled, the more his remaining blood boiled.

Our first match against Bruiser and Crusher was in January 1965, about a year after Larry and I started wrestling together. We lost that first shot at the title but came back on January 30 to take the belt from the fearsome duo. We became the youngest American Wrestling Association tag-team champions ever. I was 22, and Larry was 29.

The Crusher came up with a brilliant angle that kept the fans coming back for more every time our team wrestled theirs. One day, he showed up in the ring doing a mock impersonation of me, wearing a dress and blonde wig (I had longer bleached-blond hair at the time). He portrayed Larry and me as cross-dressing sissies, dubbing us the "Dolly Sisters." The moniker stuck, and male fans started dressing in drag at shows to mock us, while cheering for Bruiser and Crusher.

This was before the day when the wrestling companies had tight control over characters and scriptwriters to tell them what to say. The "Dolly Sisters" was as close to a storyline as wrestling had back then, and it was a huge success with the fans.

In a 1967 issue of *Wrestling Review* magazine, Crusher didn't try to hide his distain for us: "The Dolly Sisters aren't even good amateurs. Larry Hennig can't drink beer worth anything, and Harley Race goes to a hairdresser. What kind of men would do that?"

In the same article, Bruiser said: "Me and Crusher can take them Dolly Sisters any time. Gertrude Hennig and Sylvia Race are the worst excuse for rasslers you ever seen. They pay them girls to cheer them."

For our part, Larry and I portrayed Crusher and Bruiser as big, dumb beer-drinking hicks.

"Crusher and Bruiser could be great wrestlers," I was quoted as saying in that same issue of *Wrestling Review*. "They have a lot of ability, but instead of training, they spend most of their time in saloons. They are both illiterate and do not appreciate the finer things in life. They were a good team, but when they came up against the greatest team of all time, Handsome Harley Race and Pretty Boy Larry Hennig, there was no question at all that we would win the title."

Crusher had found an angle to bring the fans in, and Larry and I found a publicity stunt to get us even more attention. We entered the inaugural International 500 Snowmobile Race from Winnipeg, Canada, to St. Paul, Minnesota. The queen of England and dozens of other dignitaries were among the attendees. It was also well covered by the press—one photographer snapped a shot of Larry hoisting his snowmobile above his head.

Everything was fine until the starting gun went off and I realized I had to drive this damn thing through 500 miles of frozen wasteland. I wanted the publicity, but I quickly realized I wasn't up for the race. Despite numerous warnings to bundle up, I was dressed like I was taking a late fall walk in the park. The temperature: 47 below zero. And that was without the wind chill factor.

I rode my snowmobile about 25 miles before—thank God— it finally broke down. When a race official assured me that he would have my machine up and running in no time, I told him: "Do whatever you want with it, but I'm going to Minneapolis. To hell with this race."

Larry, who outweighed his snowmobile by 10 pounds, fared much better. He not only finished the race, but also went on to win the "survivor trophy" for overcoming various hardships along the way.

After successfully defending our title for six months, we dropped it to the newly formed team of Gagne and Crusher. Two weeks later, on August 7, we won it back and held it for nearly a year before losing to Crusher/Bruiser in May 1965. After losing a rematch shortly thereafter, we headed out for a tour of Australia and New Zealand. In June 1966, we became the first World Tag-Team champions for Australia's International Wrestling Alliance. We later dropped that belt to Mark Lewin and Dominic DeNucci.

In the fall of 1966, we returned to the United States and began our quest to win back the title. On January 6, 1967, we again took the title away from Crusher and Bruiser.

During a match on November 1, Larry was lifting his opponent, a 260-pound John Powers, when another wrestler bounced off the referee and into Larry's legs, bending them inward. As Hennig lowered Powers, one of his knees bent the wrong way at nearly a 90-degree angle, tearing the cartilage and tendons in his leg. As I watched, I knew in an instant that our on-again, off-again two-year title run was off again. It would be the last time we would own the title. Larry recovered, and our tag team was reunited in April 1968. We wrestled together for the remainder of the year before going our separate ways. Hennig kept wrestling, but his leg never completely healed.

While Hennig was recovering, the AWA teamed me with Don Stansauka, a former NFL player who turned to wrestling and changed his name to Hard Boiled Haggerty. Rather than looking like the brute you'd expect with this name, Haggerty looked more like a middle-class guy from the suburbs. But he had appeared in several movies, and he was a perfectionist. He

was a class act, but sometimes he was the kind of guy who could-
n't get along with his own mother. If you didn't measure up to
his standard of perfection, he let you know.

I often stayed at a downtown hotel in Minneapolis, and a desk
clerk at the hotel once told me the following story over a beer:
A wrestling fan found out Haggerty was staying at this hotel and
knocked on his door repeatedly. By the third time, The Hag
slapped the guy around, then threw him down a flight of steps.
He then went to the front desk and grabbed the desk clerk (the
same one telling the story), and told him, "If you ever let anyone
up to my room who I don't know again, I'll throw you right out
the front door like that guy."

After Haggerty, I was teamed with a Yugoslavian named Chris
Markoff. He didn't speak much English, and he was a short-ter-
mer, too. (Incidentally, he and Haggerty were tag-team champions without ever winning the belt. They subbed for Hennig and
me on several occasions, but the AWA let us keep the title. They
were sort of like reserve members of our tag-team.)

Hennig was the best partner I ever had. He was a gentleman
and a family man, and I can honestly say we never had an argu-
ment. But I had been there, done that with the tag-team thing. I
was ready to strike out on my own.

By this time, Sandra and I had divorced, and I had met another woman. One night, she and I were driving from Minneapolis
to visit a relative in Minnesota. I saw a Corvette scream by my
car. I then saw a bright glow up ahead. As I drove around a curve,
I saw the Corvette upside down in a ditch beside the road. The
engine was ablaze, and the fire was spreading to the back of the
car—toward the gas tank.

My own horrific car crash from 1960 was still in my head
when I slammed on the brakes and told my girlfriend to go for
help. I ran to the car and positioned my shoulders under the car
door, then somehow managed to use my leg strength to push the
car up and over on its wheels. The driver's head rolled out of the
car and over toward my feet. Still, the last thing I wanted to see
happen was his body burn up with the car, so I grabbed his

corpse and pulled it out. As I pulled him out, blood spewed from his neck onto me.

The media in Minneapolis covered the event, billing me as a hero who tried to save this man's life. The only problem with that is that I had worked for years to become a villain, and now the fans were starting to cheer for me shortly after the incident. I flipped them off and stuck out my tongue at them, but many continued to cheer.

Hennig and I quit wrestling as a team, and he formed a new tag team with Lars (Larry Heinimi) Anderson. Hennig stayed with the AWA for most of his career. As for me, I married the woman I had been dating and was headed for my second trip to Japan before looking to make my mark as a solo wrestler in the United States.

[1] Some information on Dick the Bruiser and The Crusher was derived from The Professional Wrestling Hall of Fame Web site, www.wrestlingmuseum.com

FIVE

HEEL HEAT WASN'T MEANT TO BE LIKE THIS
(BUT THE PAY'S NOT BAD)

"The first time I heard Harley's name, he had gotten stabbed in a fight at the Chestnut Tree. I wouldn't even drive by there. It's that tough a place."

—Ric Flair

I'm not a bad guy; I just played one in the ring.

Being a heel is the ultimate experience in living vicariously. You get to throw the normal rules of etiquette out the window while you strut around the ring, cheat behind the referee's back, and generally act like an egotistical SOB. And you get paid to do it.

If you do your job well, the fans will hate you so much that they'll come back to see you time and time again. But if you do your job too well, they might have more on their minds than just holding up signs and booing.

I learned this the hard way while wrestling in Tennessee in the early '60s, then in Minneapolis in the late '60s.

This was before most wrestlers entered to music, so we often got into character and worked the crowds ourselves before the bell rang. Around that time, I used to say that "I've got the body that men fear and women crave." As I walked into the ring, I would pick the best-looking woman at ringside to flirt with. With an unabashed cocky demeanor, I would flex my muscles in front of her, and say: "What's a good-looking lady like you doing with a skinny-looking geek like that?"

The act drew various reactions from the women, but the men all felt the same: They hated me. What made them even madder was that they knew I wasn't just an eye-gouging cheat—I had good technical training, and I could wrestle with the best of them.

After matches, fans often would wait for the wrestlers at the back of the areas where they just performed. Rock stars called them groupies. Wrestlers called them "arena rats," although I never did like the term. It was there where I met a young woman after a show, and we began to date.

Her father didn't like me from the get-go, and he didn't hide the fact. On several occasions, he told me to stay away from his daughter. He didn't want his daughter with a professional wrestler, and, I suspect, he especially didn't want her with one as crazy as he heard I was.

It was around this time that my "handsome" moniker was supplemented by a new one that I earned after taping a recent promo. As a publicity stunt, someone threw me a piece of raw meat, and I bit into it like a rabid animal. I then became "Mad Dog" Harley Race. During this period, I once picked up a brick during a promo and used my forearm (with help from the metal plate in it) to break it in two. Then I picked up a chunk and beat it against my forehead until blood streamed down my face.

I don't know how much this girl's father knew about me, but I suspected that he bought into my "bad guy" persona. One evening, he began shouting at me as we stood about 10 feet apart. I yelled back, but before I could get out a sentence, he had drawn a handgun and was pointing it in my general direction. Then he pulled the trigger.

I think he meant it as a warning shot, but the bullet ricocheted off the ground and struck me in the knee. I charged at him, threw a left hook to his jaw and was on top of him grabbing his gun before he could get off a second shot.

His daughter—and I believe his wife—had witnessed the event, and soon a small crowd had gathered. Fortunately, neither of us was seriously injured. I declined to press charges, but I also declined to continue dating the girl with the psycho dad.

Heel heat could be a bitch at times. As a wrestler, you have to be aware that you're playing with people's emotions. The goal is to get them just to their boiling point, then do something to cool them down a bit. By getting their blood boiling, you expect to get yelled at constantly. The taunts ranged from "you suck" to things I won't mention here. It also wasn't uncommon for people to wad up paper, spitballs or anything handy to throw at you on your way into the ring or back into the dressing room. Sometimes fans doused me with their drinks.

I would do what I could to perpetuate my bad-boy image. Once in 1969, I was taping a wrestling segment with Grizzly Smith, the father of Jake "The Snake" Roberts. Smith's gimmick was that you could punch him as hard as you wanted, and he wouldn't feel a thing. (Incidentally, Houdini had the same gimmick, and it led to his death after he was sucker-punched.) A week before, Smith told his fans: "You could even come off a 20-foot ladder onto my stomach and it wouldn't hurt me."

So during our taping, I walked into the studio and said, "I've got my 20-foot ladder. I want you in the ring."

After a commercial break, I begin climbing up the ladder, past the studio's lighting equipment, until I reached the top. Then I flung my body down as Griz nervously laid down on a mat. I landed with a "boom," dropping a knee right on his neck—nowhere close to his stomach. Griz started foaming at the mouth, then lay unconscious with his tongue hanging out while an ambulance came to load him into it. I stood there laughing at

Griz's misfortune. Meanwhile, announcer Nick Roberts was incensed, ranting into the microphone about what a "low-life human being" I was. The fans were outraged.

Tom Prichard, a wrestler-turned-talent scout for the WWE, saw the event on television when he was just a young fan, and it made a lasting impression—although probably for the wrong reason. After seeing it, his family moved to Houston, where promoter Paul Boesch was talking about how Grizzly Smith's career had possibly been ended because Johnny Valentine did an elbow drop on him from the second rope. That left a confused young Prichard wondering what really happened. After Prichard broke into the business, he asked Grizzly about the incident, and Griz said he spent his six-week recovery period on a tour of Japan. Griz told Prichard that he didn't know me very well at the time, so he was nervous about doing the stunt. But he said my knee never touched his neck, and that everything went as planned.

During our championship run, Larry and I even started getting hate mail from the fans, telling us in not-so-kind words that we were lousy wrestlers and we were neither "pretty" nor "handsome."

All this could be annoying, but up until that point, at least it was relatively harmless. I figured at least none of the fans would be so crazed as to actually attack us.

I had always heard stories of wrestlers getting attacked by fans, but it's the kind of thing you don't think will happen to you. But early in my career, it did. It was the early '60s when I was wrestling on my first tag team with John Long. We had just beaten Len Rossi and Tex Riley, and the crowd was in a frenzy. We slid through the bottom ropes and followed our police escorts toward the dressing room. As we headed through the crowd, I saw a man lunging toward me out of the corner of my eye. I reacted instinctively by throwing a punch, but it was too late. I felt a sting in my right forearm, and I looked down to see a knife sticking out of my arm. My assailant looked to be in his mid 20s, a few years older than me. At the same time his friends were helping him back to his feet, they were denying their friend stabbed me.

So I pulled the knife out of my arm and handed it to friendly Mr. Police Officer. Surely he'll handle the bad guy. "That's who stabbed me," I said, pointing to the man. But instead of making an arrest, the cop decided the best way to "protect and serve" was to throw the incident back in my face. He suggested I may have started the fight, and that—for all he knew—the knife was mine. "You're the one who handed it to me," he pointed out.

The cops' job at wrestling events is to keep the peace and serve as your protection. But they're also wrestling fans, and they buy into the "heel" bit just like other fans. I suspect this cop just thought that since I was a "bad guy" that I was asking for trouble. Once a police escort told me: "If any of this crap with the fans starts, we're not getting involved because you're the one inciting it." After that, I made it a point to introduce myself to the cops before the matches so they'd watch my back afterward.

After this stabbing incident, my first priority was to get the hell out of the arena before the incident stirred up the rest of the crowd like a beehive. I decided not to press charges to avoid spending the rest of the evening in the local ER and then filing a report at the police department. Plus, I'd have to return to testify if the case came to trial. So I went back to the locker room and gave myself what would be the royal HMO treatment these days: I flipped a loose piece of skin on my forearm back to where it was supposed to be and wrapped it in tape.

Unfortunately, it wasn't the last time I was stabbed. During my tag-team run with Hennig, a frequent Minneapolis haunt of other wrestlers ("the boys," as we say in the business) was a restaurant/bar called The Chestnut Tree. One evening, I walked into the place and noticed a guy near the cash register slapping an attractive young lady. I looked around and nobody seemed interested in getting involved. So I walked up to the guy and said, "Enough is enough. Leave her alone." He told me to mind my f•••ing business, and when he could see that I wasn't going to, he threw a punch. I fended it off, and then landed one on him before I saw a second man beside him lunging at me. I caught him in the face with a left hook that knocked him back onto the restaurant's entrance mat, opening the automatic door. I turned to see a third guy who was somehow involved, and he put up his arms as if to say: "I don't want any part of this fight." So I turned my back for a second to see whether the other two were getting back to their feet. Bad mistake. As soon as I turned, I felt a burning sensation in my back. This "innocent bystander" who just threw up his arms had pulled out a knife and stabbed me in the back as I looked away. I was injured pretty badly, but my adrenaline was flowing. And, by now, I was angry. And like that big green guy in the comics, you don't wanna see me when I'm angry.

I figured if this guy wants to use weapons, I could play that game, too. So I pulled out a handgun that I bought earlier that same day.

Before anything could come of it, the manager jumped between us. "Harley, please don't shoot!" he screamed. The three men fled and were arrested shortly after. It was only later I found out that the woman being roughed up was a prostitute, and the three men were her pimps.

The knife had hit one of my ribs and followed along the rib. If it hadn't hit the rib, it likely would have punctured my lung. As it was, I had a tube in my back for four weeks to drain the liquids. I was sidelined for 10 weeks. Promoters typically weren't patient enough to wait that long for one of their wrestlers to heal from a legitimate injury, much less a fight. Unlike baseball, you can't just be put on the disabled list. Often you'd be fired. Fortunately for me, Hennig and I were filling enough seats at our venues that they cut me some slack. They substituted Chris Markoff during my absence and then put me back with Hennig when I was ready.

During our tag-team years, Hennig was the quintessential family man. I, as you may have guessed by now, was not. This period of my life was a coming of age of sorts for me. Everyone handles fame and money in different ways. I chose to live life at the edge.

During my tag-team stint with Long in Tennessee, I was earning an average of $25 a night. In Minneapolis, I was bringing in $800 a week and spending it like a drunken sailor on leave. Like other guys, I dropped my share of money in bars and strip joints. But my real weakness was for vehicles. At various times in Minneapolis, I had four cars, two boats and 10 motorcycles.

I think my fascination with cars stemmed from when I owned my first car at the age of 15. It was a 1949 Ford. I couldn't afford antifreeze, so I drained the water out of the engine each night that winter. One night I forgot, and the water froze. When I started the car, the ice thawed and expanded, splitting the engine block.

As a kid, I never seemed to have a roadworthy car for very long. I certainly never had the kind of cars you saw advertised on TV. So when I came into money, I went all out.

I went from driving cars so old I'd worry about making it to my next show to shiny cars that were off the showroom floor. One of my first acquisitions was a 1965 Pontiac Bonneville. But not long after I bought the new convertible, I finished a wrestling match and walked out to the parking lot to find my car on fire. Again, the cops were their helpful selves. "If you weren't such an asshole, agitating these people, maybe these things wouldn't happen to you," one offered.

The crime was never solved. No doubt it was arson, and to this day I suspect it was an overzealous fan who saw me—the bad-guy wrestler—get out of the car and head inside for his match.

At a certain point you become exasperated. What could they possibly do to piss me off more than setting my car on fire?

I had towed a 16-foot boat with me to Minneapolis, then, in 1967, upgraded to a 25-foot Trojan mini-cruiser with full inboard and a V8 engine. Since the employees of the boat company knew who I was, they gave me the boat before I officially bought it. They told me I could take it out over the weekend and finish the paperwork on Monday. So I took it for a cruise, and then came back with Hennig on Monday to show him the boat and to sign the papers. When we showed up, the boat was gone. There were four ropes coming out of the water where the boat had been. We looked closer and saw my shiny new boat resting several feet under water at the bottom of Lake Minnetonka. The plugs had been pulled out. Again, it's still an unsolved crime to this day, but I suspect it wasn't random. My best guess is that someone had it out for their least favorite wrestler, yours truly. But since the boat wasn't officially mine yet, the company agreed to refurbish it and bill its insurance company.

"Heel heat" could be scorching at times. But it also made me a ton of money. And it proved beyond a shadow of a doubt that I was doing my job rather well.

Don't get me wrong. I've always viewed these incidents as isolated crimes by a few idiots. I've never had anything but appreciation for my fans. They're the ones who've paid my bills my entire life. That's something I'll never forget.

SIX

A PARTNERSHIP
IN KANSAS CITY

*"I met Harley back in 1962 in St. Joseph (Missouri)
where I was a wrestling promoter. Harley had a great
attitude. He'd try anything, had a lot of desire, and
was a tough kid. I thought he had a pretty decent
future, yes I did. Gus Karras spoke highly of him and
liked his attitude, too."*

—promoter Bob Geigel

When Larry and I parted in late 1969, I took a solo
tour in Japan for a few weeks before heading back to
California. A wrestling outfit from Japan offered me
a job to book shows out of their Los Angeles office. The head
booker was also a wrestler who went by the name Mr. Moto. But
by the time I arrived in Los Angeles, my job had already been
snatched away by one of wrestling's greatest villains.

"Classy" Freddie Blassie was a standout wrestler in the U.S.
Navy before wrestling professionally. He won the NWA
Southern Heavyweight championship in 1954, and reclaimed

the title 14 times throughout his career. He earned the nickname "The Vampire" after claiming to have filed down his teeth into fangs that he used in the ring to tear into the foreheads of his opponents. He also coined the term "pencil-neck geek," which he frequently used to describe opponents and fans alike.

Blassie's career was on the downward slope, and mine was climbing. But we did have something in common: We were both heels who had been stabbed and had cars burned to the ground by irate fans. A mob of wrestling fans once overturned and torched his brand new Cadillac.[1]

Blassie was nearing the age of 50, and he wanted a young up-and-coming wrestler for a tag-team partner to help prop up his own ticket sales. He picked me. When we wrestled together, it was yours truly who took the pinfall when our team lost. But that wasn't the problem—I knew my day in the spotlight would come. The problem was that I wasn't interested in being a tag-team partner with anyone, much less an aging star. I went there to learn the business side of wrestling. Running occasional errands for Blassie didn't count. Don't get me wrong, Blassie was very talented at what he did, and I tried to learn from him while I was there. But it was Blassie's job that I originally was hired for; it just so happened that he got there first.

I can't say my stint in Los Angeles taught me anything about booking matches, but it did get my foot in the door. After two months, I called Dory Funk Sr. and he offered me a job in Amarillo to help him book in that territory.

At the time, if you wanted to get involved in the business side of the profession, it helped to be a member of the family that ran a particular territory. But Dory hired me because he trusted me, and because he needed a break. So for the next nine months, I operated the territory along with the Funks, including Terry, who had just started his wrestling career. Meanwhile, Dory Funk Jr. was being put in line to win the NWA title from Gene Kiniski.

I had seen the business from inside the "squared circle" for a decade. Now it was time to gain some valuable office experience

by day, while continuing to wrestle by night. And when I say by
night, I mean every night. I wrestled seven days a week during
this period, with few exceptions.

To understand the business side of a particular territory back
then, it helps to understand how the business worked overall. At
the time, the NWA was a loose coalition of 28 territories across
the country. Each was owned and operated by a different indi-
vidual, family or group. But representatives of the organization
met on a regular basis to take care of certain business functions.
It also had a committee that met to determine future championship matches, as well as the champions themselves.

The only separate territory from the NWA was Washington,
D.C.-based Capitol Wrestling, which was owned by Vince
McMahon Sr. The territory was so powerful that it didn't need
the NWA, so it didn't associate itself with the group as strongly
as other territories.[2]

The NWA territories had an unwritten agreement that they
wouldn't do business in other territories, and that they would
occasionally share their own wrestlers with other promoters on
a limited basis. It was a gentleman's agreement that mostly
worked until the 1980s. But the "Decade of Greed," as it was
called, would see the end of that old-fashioned way of doing
business and the beginning of the end for the NWA.

My job running the territory included matchmaking—pairing wrestlers with similar chemistry, and putting the right
wrestlers in the right towns so that fans filled the seats. When I
arrived, there were probably four wrestlers who were keeping
the territory afloat. Three of them were the Funks: Dory, Dory
Jr. and Terry. The other was a Mexican wrestler by the name of
Ricky Romero. He was a talented wrestler and a hero in the
Texas towns heavily populated with Mexicans.

In those towns—towns such as Albuquerque, El Paso,
Littlefield, Clovis and St. Angelo—you could sell out for the
night if you paired Romero with a good wrestler who could
push him physically. I often pitted Mike DiBiase or myself against
him.

DiBiase was a national collegiate wrestling champion at the University of Nebraska. He went on to win various regional NWA titles 10 times and had notable feuds with Dory Funk Jr. and Sr. He once wrestled a one-hour, 44-minute "Texas Death Match" with Dory Sr.[3]

On July 2, 1969, Mike showed up for a match in Lubbock, Texas, after spending the better part of the day hauling furniture to move his family. He looked exhausted and his face was pale. "You look like you're worn out," I told him before his match. "You don't have to wrestle tonight. We can change things."

But Mike declined my offer. "Harley, I wouldn't be here if I didn't want to wrestle tonight," he said.

He proceeded with his match against Man Mountain Mike, a bearded brute from Montana weighing nearly 500 pounds. As I watched the match, I saw DiBiase grab his chest and fall. The referee froze, not knowing whether he should start the count. (That's part of a referee's job when someone is injured in the ring.) I ran into the ring and started administering mouth-to-mouth and CPR on DiBiase. But it was too late. He was pronounced dead at the hospital from a massive heart attack that probably started before he stepped into the ring.

His son, Ted, who was still in high school, later went on to become "The Million-Dollar Man" and have a great wrestling career of his own. I had always counted Mike as a friend, and Ted and I have always been good friends as well.

As I'm writing this, 21 wrestlers have died in the ring since the advent of professional wrestling.[4] It was the first time I had seen it happen. Unfortunately, it wouldn't be the last.

Thursdays were the biggest days of the week as far as business was concerned. It was on those days I would meet with the Funks to decide who would wrestle whom at which venue during the upcoming week. Pairing opposing wrestlers to give the most excitement to the fans was an art, and my training during this period would help me down the road.

Without my experience and the contacts I made while running the Amarillo territory, I think my path to become the world champion would have been much longer.

It was late in the summer of 1970, and I had been a nomad the better part of my life, traveling from one territory to the next. I was ready to settle down to a place I could call home. Plus, I was about to become a father. So I returned to Kansas City. On October 5, I had just returned home from a match when my wife informed me that she thought it was time to go to the hospital. I tried to convince her it was another false alarm, but she was insistent. She finally won out, and it's a good thing: Justin Michael was born a little over four hours later. It was a life-changing experience. Every man tends to want a son to be a clone of himself, and I could definitely see myself in Justin right away.

Like any parent, I wanted the best for him. Justin learned to swim before he could walk, and I was teaching him to play golf not long after that. But what I couldn't do was shelter him from the teasing and taunts he would later get in school over his father. I had to pay the price for being a heel, but my son shouldn't have had to. But kids can be mean, and he wound up taking a lot of flak for his old man.

Justin wasn't my first child. I also had a daughter with my second wife, Sandra Jones, a year after we were married in 1963. Candice Marie was born in Maryville, Missouri. Of the few regrets I've had in my life, one is that I wish I had been more of a father to her. Three years after she was born, her mother and I divorced. Forgive me if I don't dwell on my two marriages that ended in divorce. The truth is that they're painful memories.

Our family had settled in Kansas City, and by 1972, we owned our first home: an almost new 2,500-square-foot, raised-ranch house in Lenexa, Kansas.

One year later, I made another investment in our future. Heart of America was the parent company to All-Star Wrestling, a four-state wrestling territory that also aired wrestling shows by the same name. The company ownership was split into equal thirds held by Gus Karras, Bob Geigel and Pat O'Connor.

In 1973, the trio allowed me to buy into the company. Between money I already had and a small loan, I came up with the $50,000 needed to buy 10 percent of the company.

They say that the difference between renting an apartment and owning a home is the difference between paying a landlord and paying yourself. I figured wrestling had made its share of money from me; now it was my turn to start paying myself. Not that I hadn't made a good living previously, but now I could get paid to wrestle, plus earn a percentage of the All-Star Wrestling profits created in part from my own sweat and blood.

It was around this time I became the U.S. Central States Champion. The Kansas City territory started promoting me as the new titleholder. It was an honor, and a good stepping-stone for what was to come. But there was one problem: It was a title without a belt. Somewhere along the line, the belt got lost. So when I walked into the ring before the matches, I had nothing to wear, nothing to hold up to the audience. So I forked over $150 and had another one made, and billed it to All-Star Wrestling. If I was the titleholder, I was going to have a belt. That same belt now hangs on my office wall.

The Midwest wasn't one of the prized territories to work in. Many wrestlers preferred territories around Minneapolis, Georgia or the East Coast. But All-Star Wrestling had the benefit of getting good wrestlers from both coasts, even if they were just on tour here for a few months. I guess we had the right talent at the right time, because the shows started selling out at many of our venues. Plus, wrestling's popularity in general was starting to spike, and it would last for about a decade. It was a good time to invest in wrestling.

We had tons of talent: Danny Little Bear, Rufus R. Jones, Roger Kirby, "Bulldog" Bob Brown, Bob Geigel, Pat O'Connor and Ronny Etchison to name a few. Our territory's women wrestlers included Betty Nicoli, Jean Antone and Dot Dotson.

Things were going well in my life. I had wealth, fame and a family. But when I started to get too big for my own shoes, I always had the Hite sisters to put me in my place.

Mertie and Gertie Hite were eccentric little old ladies with a passion for pro wrestling. They were, in a word, fanatics. The identical twins owned a huge farm near Platte City, Missouri. How they kept up the farm, I'll never know, because they seemed to be at more wrestling matches than I was. During the '60s and '70s, you could attend pretty much any show in Topeka, Kansas, or the Missouri cities of Kansas City, St. Joseph or Sedalia, and you'd find them at ringside. They were easy to spot, because they wore identical dresses, glasses and hats, complete with long hat pins.

The Hite sisters became almost famous at wrestling matches, but they shunned the attention. They would cringe if a ring announcer tried to advertise their presence. I still own a picture that a photographer took of them at ringside, and both of them are looking at the ground.

Ironically, they were anything but shy ladies when the matches started. And they weren't afraid to use those hat pins of theirs. Me being the area's big meanie, I think I was on the receiving end of their pokes more than any other wrestler. These weren't playful jabs, either. If I made the mistake of wrestling out of the ring near them, I could expect to make a small blood donation. If I kept my distance, they'd be limited to shaking their purses and umbrellas at me. Some fans said they could be heard screaming words that would make even us wrestlers blush, although I never heard a profane word from either of them. Of course, there wasn't much I could do to defend myself from them. It's not like I was going to haul off and slug them, so I just tried to avoid them as best I could. Even security treated them with kid gloves, often just scolding them while trying to keep a straight face.

After taking the sisters' money for years to see Kansas City-area wrestling shows, Geigel—normally a shrewd businessman—stopped charging them. What was he thinking? So not only did they get lifetime memberships to All-Star Wrestling, but they

probably also considered it a green light to continue hounding
me with their hat pins.

[1] Information on Blassie taken from *The Complete Idiot's Guide to Pro Wrestling* and
www.wrestlingmuseum.com.

[2] Information on the NWA and the territories taken from *The Complete Idiot's Guide
to Pro Wrestling*, second volume.

[3] www.obsessedwithwrestling.com

[4] *The Complete Idiot's Guide to Pro Wrestling*, second edition

SEVEN

WORLD CHAMP: A SHORT STINT AT THE TOP

"Harley Race went out there every night and gave his best, and took bump after bump after bump. It was Harley's attitude that whether there is 5,000 people or 50, he said, 'You give your best every time. Those 50 come when there is four feet of snow on the ground; they deserve your best.' That's the attitude Harley had."

—Ted DiBiase

By 1973, Dory Funk Jr. had been the World Heavyweight Champion for nearly four years, and the NWA's decision makers were ready for a changing of the guard. But Funk was a great champion, and his father held quite a bit of sway in the NWA. So making the switch to a new champion wasn't going to be easy.

Of course, Dory Sr. didn't want his son to lose the belt at all. Through his influence, he was able to extend Dory Jr.'s title run, but he knew the end was near. Besides, the job of being the

World Champion is like being the head coach of a professional football team—you work long hours, the burnout rate is high, and your job is always on the line. Wrestling had already taken its toll on the Funk family. That's part of the reason Dory Sr. hired me to help run the Amarillo territory three years before.

It's typical for champions to have clauses built into their contracts that give them a say as to who they pass the belt to, when the time comes. So when the NWA's nine-member championship selection committee voted to give the title to Jack Brisco, the Funks objected. Dory Sr. didn't want his son losing to one of the top babyfaces in the country. The thought was that letting a heel champ lose to a fellow heel is more respectable than having him drop the belt to a babyface, who could be perceived to be the weaker opponent. Dory Jr. wasn't so much into the politics of it—he was ready to give up the title because he didn't want to lose his family to wrestling. The cross-country traveling that comes with being the top dog wasn't helping matters.

Two of the selection committee members, Eddie Graham out of Florida and LeRoy McGuirk out of Tulsa, Oklahoma, were pushing hard for Brisco to get the title.

An agreement was struck that the belt would be passed from Dory Jr. to Brisco, but by way of another wrestler. That way, Dory Jr. wouldn't have to lose it to babyface Brisco, but Brisco would still soon be the champ. Everyone was happy, including me when I found out that I was picked as the go-between champion.

I first heard that I was in line to become the champion about a month before it happened. I was excited, sure, but I can't say I actually jumped for joy or anything. In wrestling, everything's tentative until it happens. I didn't get my hopes up until I knew for sure the title was headed my way. (Although that would be my mistake the next time around.) Because of the internal squabbles, the title switch was probably delayed at least eight months. The match was held on May 24, 1973, in Kansas City. The match itself doesn't really stand out in my mind. Dory Jr. and I had wrestled each other dozens of times. This was really no different. Only, this time, I would walk away with 10 pounds of gold around my waist.

The match lasted about a half-hour and ended after I pushed Funk into the referee, who then administered the count on Funk after I pinned him. After the match, Funk groused in interviews that, if not for the interference involving the referee, he never would have lost the belt. Of course, he knew differently, but it sounded good.

I had won other titles before, including the tag-team championship with Hennig, but this was different. At the time, the NWA was *the* wrestling organization. If you won the NWA Heavyweight Championship belt, you were essentially the undisputed World Heavyweight Champion. Even though I knew that I wouldn't be the champion long, winning it that first time was the most exhilarating point in my professional career.

The plan originally was to have me lose the title within weeks. But because the selection committee was happy with the crowd response I got, they extended my run to two months. By traveling across the United States defending my title during that period, I transformed myself from a respected regional wrestler to a top worldwide talent. The NWA probably covered half the planet. It probably had at least 500 wrestlers under its umbrella. For the first time, I was at the top. It was a huge break in my career that gave me more experience, more exposure, and more money.

That short stint of being the champion tested me in a way I hadn't anticipated. I knew I'd have to travel around the country defending my title. What I didn't know is that some of the territories would put me up against men who, quite frankly, couldn't wrestle their way out of a paper bag. So my challenge was to make it appear to the audience that these guys could actually hold their own with me. After wrestling enough of these journeymen, I started to pride myself on being able to wrestle a mop and make the mop look like it's whipping my ass.

Shortly after I took the belt, I was sent to Nashville to wrestle the son of Nick Goulas, who was a promoter there at the time. His son, George, wasn't cut out to be a wrestler, but his father encouraged him nonetheless. So when George showed up that night to wrestle the world champ, he was horrified. And to top it off, we were scheduled to go for an hour.

There was a group of regular fans in the area that knew the only reason George was a wrestler was because of his dad. And they often sat toward the front and let him know that they knew. They jeered and taunted him as he wrestled.

Well, that night they saw a transformation in a young man. George didn't beat me, but for most of the match I made it appear as if he could. And after the match was over, George used his newfound courage to confront four of these hecklers who he previously feared. He even wound up slapping one of them.

The dispute between George and the fans continued back in the dressing room. One of the guys punched George, and then Nick punched his son's assailant. The problem was, Nick didn't pack much more of a punch than George; neither one could break an egg with their fists. So I decked the heckler, who lay unconscious until the referee came back and threw a glass of water in his face.

Shortly afterward, Nick came up to me and thanked me for taking care of his son both in and out of the ring. "That's what I get paid to do," I replied. Then he shocked me by handing me three $100 bills, which I graciously accepted. Nick was the kind of man who was a good talker, and always acted like business took a backseat to friendship. But as long as you knew it was the other way around, you could get along with the guy. So I had to laugh when, several days later, I received my check for wrestling that night. It was for my standard fee, minus $300.

My run as titleholder seemed to end as soon as it began. A taste of success at such a high level was great, but it whet my appetite for more. On July 20, however, I focused on the job at hand: boosting the name Jack Brisco into superstar status.

In reality, Brisco didn't need much help. He was a four-time NCAA national wrestling champion for the Oklahoma Sooners who also played on the football team. The six-foot, 230-pound mat technician entered the pro wrestling ranks after college. His natural talent and All-American looks impressed the fans, while his workmanlike attitude and ability to earn money impressed the promoters. He was probably the purest babyface to carry the NWA strap.

About 11,500 fans showed up to the San Houston Coliseum in Houston, Texas, to watch the showdown. Before and after the match I talked privately with Jack. I had no problem dropping the belt to him. I knew that was the plan all along, and that I was just fortunate enough to get it for a short time. I congratulated Jack and told him that he was finally getting the belt he deserved.

When I walked into the ring with the NWA World Heavyweight Championship belt that night, I would be the last person to wear that belt in the ring. The match started with a belt exchange—the old belt was retired and replaced with a new NWA belt that included more flags from different countries.

The match itself was designed to make Brisco look like he was on the receiving end of an ass kicking up until the end.

We hadn't wrestled each other much previously, but our wrestling styles matched up well since we both liked a lot of technical wrestling down on the mat.

The match lasted about 25 minutes, and by the end there weren't three people in the building who thought Brisco had a chance of winning. For one, I had just recently won the belt and many fans didn't expect me to lose it so soon. Plus, I had the upper hand pretty much throughout the match, just as we planned.

Near the end, I jumped off the top rope to land across his body. But Jack pulled up his knees and my chest landed right into them, knocking the wind out of me. As soon as I stood up, he was coming off the ropes. He jumped into me with a flying body press (also known as a Thez body press, after Lou Thez). In one sweeping motion, he slammed into my body, knocking me backward, while trapping my arms above my head and grapevining my legs as I fell on my back. That's when he got the count: 1-2-3.

The shocked crowd cheered. Brisco was the new NWA Champion.

My championship run was followed up by another kind of fight—a turf war. I was brought into the Atlanta territory in late summer of 1973 as a booker for promoter Jim Barnett. Ray Gunkle had recently died, and there was a raging battle to control that territory. When Ray died, no one expected his wife, Ann, would want to continue the operation. Barnett came into the territory after he died, hoping to buy out the family's share's from his widow. But Ann was a driven woman, and she was determined to stay in the wrestling business, even if it meant putting up a fight.

I replaced Louis Tillet, who trained me for about a month before leaving. When he did, there were some people in the Gunkle organization who wanted to make sure I didn't succeed. If I succeeded, they'd fail. Their wrestlers routinely picketed our shows, grousing that Barnett was trying to put Gunkle out of business. One night Thunderbolt Patterson—a wrestler whom I knew well, and previously had no beef with—went too far with some of the things he yelled at me. So I spit in his face to see if that would incite him to throw the first punch. Instead, he simply talked tough, telling everyone there what he was going to do to me. Finally, I said, "Put up or shut up. If you think you can take me, you can face me in the ring tonight."

When he continued to mouth off, I told the cops: "If he's not going to do anything other than talk, let's get him off the premises so he's not blocking the door." The cops escorted him away, and that was that.

It wasn't unusual for wrestlers who were either trying to break into the business or make names for themselves to come into the Atlanta office and ask me for work. These days, wrestlers often have videotapes of themselves to send to promoters. But back then, promoters would say, "Let's go to the ring and see what you know." The only problem was that, during the middle of the turf war, I didn't know who I could trust. I had reason to believe that some of the wrestlers coming to my office for tryouts were actually turncoats who worked for the Gunkle family with the intent of sabotaging our organization. So for about a month during this time, every kid who came in looking for work ended up leaving after a tryout that he wouldn't soon forget. I took them in the ring and roughed them up good enough that they would think twice about ever crossing me. I suspect some of the kids deserved it, while others were simply in the wrong place at the wrong time.

Speaking of being in the wrong place at the wrong time, it was during my stint in Atlanta that I had a reunion of sorts with my old partner, Larry Hennig. Only this reunion wasn't under the best of circumstances. We were wrestling in Florida one night, and I had just won a match against a popular foreign wrestler—maybe from Mexico or Puerto Rico. Some of the fans from his country in the front row didn't like the fact that I won, and they started mouthing me. Being the man of exceptional restraint that I am, I, of course, shot back with some insults of my own. I basically told them that I kicked their favorite wrestler's ass up and down the ring for a half hour. Pretty soon several of them were entering the ring after a piece of me. Hennig had wrestled earlier and was watching as the situation escalated from words to blows. Before long, I saw Larry jump into the ring holding a sock that was partially wrapped around his fist and dangling down with something inside. I watched as Larry ran up to one of them and swung it. The sock ricocheted off the guy's head like a slingshot and nailed Larry right in the nose, breaking it.

After we cleared the ring and headed back to the dressing room, I said: "What in the hell did you put in there?" He opened the sock and pulled out a hockey puck. I looked up at this 320-pound muscleman with blood flowing down across his lips, and laughed.

"What were you thinking? Those things are like super balls when they aren't frozen," I told him. Larry had just come to my defense, but I couldn't help but laugh at the big guy. To this day, he still reminds me sacrificed his nose to save my ass.

EIGHT

JUMPING THE PUDDLE TO JAPAN

"He's basically a living legend in Japan."
—Ken Hirayama, U.S. and foreign affairs representative
for Japan's Pro-Wrestling Noah

In 1967, I was first approached about doing a wrestling tour in Japan. Accepting it was one of the smartest moves of my career, as well as my personal life. I'm not the sentimental type of guy, but I will say this: Japan and its people have always held a special place in my heart. Some of the finest people I've met both in and out of this business have been from Japan, and I'm proud to count many of them as my friends. This chapter focuses on just a few of my memories of the country and its people.

As crazy as American fans are for wrestling, the Japanese are even more fanatic. I should know—I've made the 13,000-mile round trip some 71 times throughout my career. As of this writing, I'm planning yet another wrestling-related trip to the Far East.

About the time Hennig had injured his leg while we were tag-team partners, Crusher returned from a tour of Japan, and he spoke well of his experience there. One of the Japanese organizers of his tour asked him if he could recommend any other American wrestlers to make another tour there. Despite his reputation and despite our in-ring rivalry, Crusher could actually be a pretty good guy. We didn't associate much outside of the ring (being rivals, it would have been forbidden). But we were friendly to each other, and he respected me, so he recommended me to the promoter.

I jumped at the chance. The Japanese didn't accept "wannabes" or "could-bes." They only took U.S. wrestlers who were stars or who had that potential. Wrestlers from the United States knew this, and we considered it an honor to be invited there for a tour. Plus, I had heard the money wasn't bad. Instead of giving wrestlers a percentage of the ticket sales, they gave us flat fees that typically amounted to more than we'd make in the states for the same work. They also paid for our flight and hotel, and they assigned someone to not only drive us around and serve as a translator, but to help carry our bags. Often they would give this task to a young, up-and-coming Japanese wrestler.

I went on that first trip with Dick Murdock, Buddy Austin, and a couple other guys. The first things that struck me were the height difference between the Japanese and Americans (Americans are about five inches taller, on average), and the fact that they were so polite. In New York City, you fend for yourself while jostling for position on the streets and subways. In Japan, it's even more crowded on the streets, but people went out of their way to make a path for you.

Of course, the food was a change, too. A typical meal consisted of vegetables including white radishes stir-fried in light oil. If there was any protein in the dish, it was usually seafood. I enjoyed Japanese cuisine, but I always knew that one of the world's best steaks wasn't far away. Japan is known for its Kobe beef, made from cattle massaged with sake and fed a diet rich in grain and beer. It makes for some of the most tender, full-flavored meat you'll ever bite into. It also costs upwards of $100 a pound in today's currency for a prime cut.

Another difference I noticed right away was how the Japanese media treat wrestling compared to the U.S. media. To understand the difference, you first need to know a little history of pro wrestling journalism in America. In the United States, the mainstream media covered wrestling as a sport until 1911.

In 1908, during the "match of the century," George Hackenschmidt quit two hours into his Chicago match with Frank Gotch after complaining of dirty tactics by Gotch. Among other things, he said Gotch soaked his body with oil so he would be all but impossible to grab onto. Hackenschmidt campaigned for a rematch and got one in 1911. But before the match Gotch's people planted someone in Hackenschmidt's training camp to injure him. It was sort of a preview of the 1994 Tonya Harding – Nancy Kerrigan incident, except that Gotch's camp made it look like an accident. Hackenschmidt, who would limp for the rest of his life, tried to call off the match. Promoters said it was too late to cancel, so Hackenschmidt agreed to a compromise: He would lose the match if Gotch would let him save face by getting one of the three pinfalls. Gotch, however, double-crossed Hackenschmidt, quickly pinning him twice for the win. After the media got wind of the shenanigans, many newspapers and radio stations stopped covering wrestling as a sport.[1]

Japan, however, still covers wrestling as more of a sport. I found that out when, directly off the airplane, we were routinely ushered into a room at the airport for a news conference. Typically, about 20 members of the media—both news and sports reporters—would ask questions for 15-20 minutes. The questions ranged from "What approach will you take to defeat your opponent?" to "How do you train?" They always seemed to focus on the positive. The U.S. media, on the other hand, tends to view wrestling with more cynicism, focusing on use of steroids among wrestlers or the "secrets" of pro wrestling.

Despite being known for their politeness, the Japanese could occasionally lose their cool. It was one such occasion that gave me the kind of publicity boost that you can't get from paid advertising. During a news conference in the late '60s in Japan, I was taking questions, but apparently overlooked one reporter who was desperately trying to get my attention.

At the time, I had started to go by "Handsome" Harley Race in the states, but it hadn't really caught on yet in Japan. So the reporter, frustrated that he wasn't able to get in his question, stood up and yelled: "Handsome, I'm talking to you!" All the other members of the press corps, slightly embarrassed but amused, turned to look, then scribbled "handsome" down in their notebooks. The next day, the word "handsome" was in the headlines. Ever since then, the Japanese have known me as "Handsome" Harley Race.

During my trips to Japan, a longstanding rivalry started between Japan's top wrestler and me. Shohei Baba started his professional athletic career as a professional baseball player in Japan. But in 1960, at the age of 22, he switched to professional wrestling and called himself Giant Baba. A year later, he started making trips to the United States to wrestle. At six feet, 11 inches tall and weighing 330 pounds, he was a giant by any standards, but even more so in Japan, where the average height is about 5'5"—four inches shorter than in the United States. Baba wasn't known for being muscular, but what he lacked in muscle he made up for in endurance and stamina. He could go up to 90 minutes on the mat, and he reportedly wrestled more consecutive bouts than any other wrestler without taking time off for sickness or injury. From 1960 to 1984, he wrestled 3,764 matches in Japan alone.[2]

Baba was their Superman. After I dropped the title to Brisco in 1973, Baba won it from him in 1974. He was the first Japanese wrestler to win the NWA World Heavyweight title.

Even during wrestling matches, Japanese fans were the most polite people in the world. They focused intently on the matches, but they remain seated and, for the most part, reserved. Although I was a heel, they never booed me. I, in turn, treated them with respect.

Sometimes when we wrestled, Baba would catch me with a chop big enough to hear a "WHAP!" back in the cheap seats, and the crowd would go wild. And by wild, I mean they would say "Oooooh!" in unison, and then start a low chant of "Ba-ba, Ba-ba." Put it this way: A spilled drink now and then was all the security detail had to worry about. The fans' reserved nature was a welcome change from the heel heat I got in Minneapolis in the '60s.

Baba and I respected each other, and we became fast friends. Since Baba and I wrestled each other, we weren't supposed to socialize with each other. It was forbidden in Japan just like in America. But we ignored the unwritten rule. It didn't seem to matter when the Japanese media or fans saw us together. I think they looked at it like two athletes from different teams going for a beer after the game. It was no big deal, and, if anything, a sign of respect for each other.

Baba knew that I loved golfing, so we often were seen out on the links around Tokyo. I even bought a set of clubs and left them in Japan so I'd have a set to play with on future visits. Baba was a decent golfer who shot in the mid to low 80s usually. In my prime, I was a six-handicap player myself. Our competitive spirit led us to place bets, often 10,000 yen ($88) a hole. After 18 holes, sometimes I'd be up a few hundred and sometimes he would. But you'd be surprised at how well you can concentrate when the stakes are higher than a few beers.

Often we'd play in a foursome with other wrestlers. Sometimes Baba and I would play against Stan Hansen and "Destroyer" Dick Beyers. Baba typically paid our green fee, so one day I offered. "Baba, every time we play, you end up paying. This time it's on me."

"You don't want to do that," Baba warned. But I insisted. After all, how much can green fees set you back? When it was time to pay the bill for our foursome, I realized what a good friend Baba was to have paid all those previous times. As I took out my wallet, I started to make the conversion into U.S. dollars in my head. It was $1,600! The expression on my face was probably similar to when I was dazed by one of Baba's clotheslines in the ring.

That was the first and last time I offered to pay green fees in Japan. But whenever Baba came to the United States to wrestle, I not only insisted that he stay at my home, but I made sure we found time to hit the links at the course adjacent to my back yard in Kansas City. Right behind my back yard was the 10th tee of Leewood South Golf Course. Unfortunately, as I gained popularity, finding time to golf became harder and harder.

Early in this book, I told you that I once wrestled with my identity hidden. It was in the late '60s in Amarillo. I wrestled Baba while wearing a body suit from the waist up, and a mask covering my face. I don't recall the name I went by that night.

There aren't too many people on the planet I would have done that for, but I did it as a favor for Baba. At the time, Baba had quit Japan Pro Wrestling to form his All-Japan Pro Wrestling organization. Dory Funk Sr. became the liaison for Baba's new organization in America.

I wanted to help Baba and his new organization, but wrestling for it would have gotten me in hot water. That's because I was going to Japan regularly for his competition. Hence the mask. The reason we threw in the upper body suit was to cover the tattoos on my arms. To complete the charade, I wrestled right-handed. Since I'm a lefty, wrestling that way would have been a dead giveaway. Anyway, I wrestled Baba in that crazy outfit. The match was taped and shown in Japan, and no one ever recognized me.

During a trip to Japan in the early '70s, I befriended a young wrestler from Tonga named Uliuli Fitita. He went by the name "The Tonga Kid," then changed his name to Haku. Younger wrestling fans might know him better as his third incarnation: Meng. He switched to the latter name in 1995, when he joined World Championship Wrestling. He made his pro debut in 1977 and used the "savate kick," and, later in his career, the "Tongan death grip" as his finishing moves.

In Japan, kids who were trying to break into professional wrestling would be assigned to established American wrestlers to act as their assistant during their tours there. Baba assigned Haku to me during one of my early trips to Japan. Haku carried my bags and helped me order food among other things. The idea was for me to have an assistant and translator, and for him to learn English. Only, he got the short end of the learning stick because I guess I didn't teach him too much English. Haku was with me pretty much around the clock, but he jokes that the only English phrase he learned is: "You're doing great, kid."

One night on my first trip to Japan, I went for a beer at a bar/restaurant after a match with Murdock. Not much later, a liquored-up Buddy Austin walked in. Austin was a phenomenal wrestler, and he helped train me when I was getting into the business. But he also enjoyed his beer, and he could be a real jerk when he had enough in him. Austin had already been to Japan numerous times, and I think he saw himself as the elder states-man and Murdock as the jobber—the constant loser whose role is to boost the stature of more promising wrestlers. So Austin started ribbing Murdock and pushing him around. Murdock was a tough guy who could throw one of the hardest punches you've ever seen, but he took the abuse without attempting to retaliate. Finally, I said, "Buddy, knock that out, or I'm gonna knock you out." He chose the latter. We literally had to pull his head out of the sheetrock in the wall. Even then, he was still out cold. Until then, we never knew he had false teeth. Several of them broke when my fist hit him in the mouth. He spent the remaining three weeks in Japan getting another custom pair of teeth made. We ended up carrying Austin back to the hotel room that night. The next morning, he didn't remember exactly what happened. He just knew that he screwed up somewhere along the way, and that now he needed new teeth.

During one trip to Japan during the 1980s, the band Culture Club was just hitting it big. I've never been a fan of their music—or pop or rock music in general—but how could you not recognize Boy George when you sit next to him in the first-class section of the plane?

And if by chance I didn't know, his bodyguard was there to remind me. "That seat is taken," the bodyguard informed me. What he apparently didn't know was that it was my assigned seat, and it was taken by me. I told him as much, but as Boy George was returning from the bathroom and I got up to let him in his seat, the bodyguard grabbed me by the shoulders. "I'm escorting George to Tokyo," he said.

"I don't care what you're doing," I replied. "It's none of my business. What is my business is this seat was assigned to me, and I'm sitting here." As the bodyguard reached to grab me again, I stood up and slapped him across the face. "I'm only going to tell you one more time..." I continued.

George then stood up and interrupted me. "I think Mr. Race will do just fine sitting here," he said. "I feel perfectly safe with him escorting me to Tokyo." The bodyguard backed off, and I eased back into my seat. It was probably an interesting sight for the passengers who saw Boy George and Harley Race sitting side by side, but, as it turned out, he was a really nice guy and we got along great.

In ancient Japan, when a samurai warrior won his seventh fight, he was legally declared a god in Japan. When I won my seventh title, the Japanese pronounced me a "god of wrestling." To this day, in addition to "Handsome Harley Race," many Japanese wrestling fans refer to me as "Mr. Pro Wrestling."

[1] *Pro Wrestling: From Carnivals to Cable TV* and *The Complete Idiot's Guide to Pro Wrestling*, Second Edition.

[2] Some information about Giant Baba was taken from *Pro Wrestling: From Carnivals to Cable TV* by Keith Elliot Greenberg.

NINE

FORMER CHAMP FOREVER?

"Harley was the toughest guy in the ring and out. He feared no man and was afraid of nothing. He'd fight anybody at the drop of a hat—one guy, two guys, three guys. At the same time, he was very sensitive to people he liked. But you had to earn his respect. When he walked into the dressing room, everybody knew who he was. If he liked you, he'd shake your hand. If he didn't, he didn't say shit to you."

—Ric Flair

It was winter 1972, and Ray "The Crippler" Stevens and I had just flown from Kansas City into Omaha, Nebraska, and rented a car. Stevens was a successful wrestler who had been tag-teaming with Nick Bockwinkle and was managed by Bobby "The Brain" Heenan. By the end of his career, he would rack up a handful of titles, including three NWA tag-team titles and four AWA tag-team titles. Stevens and I met up with a few other wrestlers in Hastings, Nebraska, before making the drive to

Denver that night. Vern Gagne's son Greg and several babyfaces rode in one car, and Stevens, another heel, and I took the other rental car. The wrestler who joined us hadn't been out of college long. He had boyish looks and white hair. He offered his hand and introduced himself: "My name's Ric Flair," he said.

Before we ventured out into the Rockies, we stopped by a gas station to pick up two cases of beer and a fifth of blackberry brandy. I was driving, Stevens was riding shotgun and Flair was in the back seat.

I took a big swig of the brandy, then took a marker and marked where on the bottle the brandy went up to. I then handed the bottle to Stevens, who did the same. Stevens handed the bottle to Flair, who tried to excuse himself. "Not so fast, kid. This is how you get in the business," I told him. Flair reluctantly grabbed the bottle.

Stevens glanced at the speedometer and yelled, "Slow down, or I'm gonna sucker punch you."

Of course, anyone who has driven with me knows that getting from point A to point B doesn't include scenic stops, or, if I can help it, bathroom stops. Just me, a map with a direct route and a heavy foot. So telling me to slow down just reminded me to speed up. "Go ahead and punch me. We'll go over the cliff together," I told him, pressing my foot down even harder.

We made it through a snowstorm in the Rockies and into Denver in one piece, although the rough ride and the hard liquor had taken its toll on the young Flair. As we pulled into our hotel, Flair's snow-covered head was hung out the window and he was heaving his guts out onto the pavement. Ric was now one of the boys. Little did I know that night that he'd go on to become one of the best pro wrestlers in history.

I did a lot of stupid things when I was younger, and the previous story highlighted one of the biggest. In the '60s and '70s, wrestlers drove from one show to another more than they do now, and it wasn't uncommon for wrestlers to drink on the road. These days, tougher laws and publicity campaigns have created more of a stigma against drinking and driving. As a result, wrestlers, and society in general, have wised up to the dangers. I've driven more miles drunk then some people drive in a lifetime. I still have a heavy foot at times, but I don't drive like I'm bulletproof anymore. These days, I won't drive under the influence of anything stronger than my morning coffee.

After dropping the title to Brisco, I worked in the Atlanta office for several months. The experience allowed me to produce the wrestling show for a new nationwide television station: Turner Broadcasting Station. It also allowed me to wrestle on the East Coast, which helped establish my name in the one area of the country where I hadn't previously wrestled. Plus, I met wrestling promoters and other people in the business who I wouldn't otherwise have had the chance to meet.

Ted Turner was among those people. It was around this time that Turner's TBS station had gone nationwide, and wrestling was a big part of the original programming. The station needed content, and wrestling was a perfect fit. It was cheap to produce, and the ratings were high. But it put pressure on all of us in the Atlanta office to ensure that the matches were top notch. Our first meeting wasn't particularly memorable. I saw Turner around the TBS station several times, and we said 'hi' to each other from time to time.

I do remember when Turner first made an impression on me. He had married Jane Fonda, and the couple had moved to Montana. Some executives at TBS wanted to take wrestling off the station, and they were meeting in Atlanta to discuss the possibility. I think Jim Barnett must have called Turner to tell him, because he showed up unexpectedly. Barnett and I were in the meeting, fighting with several network brass to keep wrestling on the air. Turner walked into the boardroom, and everyone fell silent.

"I hear somebody is thinking about removing wrestling from TBS," he said. Everyone was fixated on Turner, but no one said a word. So he continued: "There's only one person in my company who's going to make that decision, and that's me. And it's not going to happen." That was the end of the discussion.

It was then I realized Turner wasn't just an independent thinker, but someone who stood up for his beliefs. He had some smart people working for him, but they were getting ready to make a bad decision. Wrestling and TBS were well suited for each other at the time, and Turner was willing to fly back to Atlanta to make sure his employees knew that, also.

After several months in Atlanta, I again returned to Kansas City. But it was a short homecoming.

In the early morning of February 20, 1975, a single-engine Cessna flying from Miami to Tampa had crashed into Hillsboro Bay close to its landing point after hitting a sudden line of clouds and thunderstorms. On board were four wrestlers: Buddy Colt, the pilot, and his tag-team partner Bobby Shane; "Playboy" Gary Hart and "Iron" Mike McCord. Shane was in the back seat and drowned. The others lived, but Colt's injuries essentially ended his career.

At the time, Eddie Graham was running the Tampa office but had hired Shane to help. Graham was at a point in his life where he wanted to slow down. After the wreck, Eddie called me, asking if I could help run the Tampa office. I proved myself trustworthy in my previous stints as a booker, and they knew I had the experience to run the Tampa office. As a booker, I tried never to use the power of the position to promote myself over other wrestlers. That might boost me as a wrestler in the short run, but in the long run it would better serve me and everyone if I made decisions based on business and not my own personal agenda.

I stayed in Tampa, booking and wrestling, just shy of a year. Accepting that job, just like accepting other booking jobs, was done with a purpose. Ever since I lost the NWA World Title in '73, everything I did was based on one goal: getting it back. I knew I had the wrestling ability to be a champion and the fan base to be a financial champ for the NWA. But I also knew that you can't wait on luck—you have to make your own. I knew that one way to increase my chance of getting back the belt was by wrestling in as many different places as possible. That way, fans in every territory knew who Harley Race was when I came to their city.

Working as a booker in different territories allowed me to wrestle in and around those territories more. It also gave me the opportunity to get to know various promoters, some of whom had votes on the championship selection committee. By showing them who I was as a wrestler, a businessman, and just a person, I knew I could further my career.

They say that opportunity only knocks once. But I always had enough confidence in myself to know that my time would come again. Still, it was trying when others started questioning whether I was a one-hit wonder. The ribbing started in the mid 1970s, first by the boys themselves. "Hey champ. Oh, wait, you were only the champ for a couple months, weren't you?" Soon, the wrestling media began wondering aloud whether I was going to remain one of the briefest champions in NWA history. Not even the fans would cut me some slack. At the beginning of matches, when they introduced me as the former world champion, they'd scream: "But for how long?!"

I never felt like I had to prove anything. A former champion is like a former Marine—the term "former" doesn't apply. But I was driven by a competitive spirit and the confidence of knowing I had what it takes to be the best.

In the meantime, Brisco was cementing his own name as a great champion by defending the title in the United States and abroad. Brisco held the belt for more than two years, with the exception of one week in December 1974, when Baba won it in Japan.

In late 1975, I got the news that I had been anxiously anticipating: I was in line to replace Brisco as the champion. Eager to see the fruits of my labor, I quit the booking job in Tampa and headed back to my Kansas City home. Finally, my dry spell had ended. I was going to be the next World Heavyweight Champion.

Only it didn't happen. On December 10, 1975, Terry Funk won the belt from Brisco in Miami. The NWA had changed its decision. Did I do something wrong? Was all my work for nothing? No, I told myself. It was a setback, nothing more. So I held my head high, and kept plugging away.

When Funk won the title, he never intended to keep it for a long time. His plan was to get in, kick some major ass and make some money, and get out. And that's what he did.

Funk made his mark during the 18 months that he had the title, but that was only the beginning. "Terrible" Terry Funk went on to become a hardcore legend that towers over his six-foot-one stature. He's lost countless quarts of blood in barbed-wire matches and nearly blown himself to smithereens in matches featuring C-4 explosives in the ring. He became known for his "moonsaults," backward somersaults from the top turnbuckle onto his opponents.

After one and a half years on the road, Funk was eager to get back to his Doublecross Ranch. Once again, it was time for the NWA officials to pass the belt. Once again, I was waiting in the wings, ready and willing to carry the NWA banner. But politics often enter the NWA's decision-making process, and I wasn't about to enter that fray. Luckily, others were.

Vince McMahon Sr. was a powerful and respected promoter of the northeast territory. By 1979, his operation would splinter from the NWA to become the World Wide Wrestling Federation (WWWF), now known as World Wrestling Entertainment (WWE).

Vince Sr. wasn't on the NWA's championship selection committee, but he wasn't afraid to use his influence when he felt strongly about something. Members of the committee later relayed to me what he told them at the time. In a speech to the committee, which was divided on who should get the belt, Vince Sr. reportedly went to bat for me. I was told he said something to the effect of: "I think this kid deserves a shot at this, and the opportunity to take the belt and run with it."

Whatever he said, it worked. The committee needed five of the nine members to agree on a new champion. I was told later that I was the unanimous choice of the committee.

The match took place on February 6, 1977, in Toronto, Canada. After some 30 minutes, Funk went for the pin by using his trademark finishing move: the spinning toehold. But I was able to reverse the hold, and put him in an Indian death lock. He surrendered in the middle of the ring, giving me the win by submission.

In winning, I became the only champion to take the belt from a pair of brothers: Dory and Terry Funk.

Funk was glad to get his life back, and I was ready to sacrifice part of mine for the only career I had ever known.

TEN

HARDCORE FEUDS AND FRIENDSHIP WITH THE FUNKSTER

"Harley was the kind of guy who would do anything for the business, if necessary. I did, too. It was important to have believability, because we went back to the same places time after time. Sometimes believability went to the extent of (taking bumps) the hard ways, which Harley did. I've done it, too; it's not a very pleasant feeling."

—Terry Funk

P ain is temporary. Pride is forever.
That could sum up the attitude Terry Funk and I shared toward wrestling. Scheduling a match between us to switch the title seemed appropriate. Since the late 1960s, Funk and I wrestled each other for money, for fun and for bloodsport. But pride was the main reason we tied each other into pretzels and bashed each other senseless time and time again.

We probably wrestled each other hundreds of times. And in those matches, we dished out and absorbed more pain for our profession than many of our contemporaries combined. But even during our most brutal feuds, when we were taking crazy bumps from each other, we always remained friends.

Watching us in or out of the ring was like watching two brothers double-dog daring each other to do something increasingly more insane.

Once Funk and I were wrestling in Japan, and Funk wanted to prove to me that anything I could do, he could do better. At the time, I was performing a move in which I'd take a bump into the turnbuckle and do a complete backflip to the floor. So during our match, as I threw Funk into the turnbuckle, he whispered: "Watch this." He hit it upside down and backwards, and then landed on the top of his head, temporarily paralyzing the left side of his face. The crazy bastard still finished the match.

In our matches against each other, we've spilled each other's blood countless times, and we've literally scarred each other for life. We upped the ante in danger by holding cage matches, barbed wire matches, Texas death matches, strap matches and chain matches. During most of the 1970s, Funk and I seemed to specialize in these crazy-ass novelty matches. Fans love the matches, because it's almost a guarantee they'll see us in our crimson masks by the time it's over.

In a chain match or Indian strap match, there's no disqualification. The combatants are connected by a 12-foot leather strap or chain. To win, you must tag all four corners while dragging the chain (and your opponent) along with you. Any offensive contact by your opponent requires you to restart the sequence. During one such match, Funk got behind me and wrapped the chain around my head, and proceeded to saw it back and forth against my face. I turned my neck back and forth with the flow of the chain to minimize the damage. But a link of the chain caught onto the skin under my eye, and it ripped my face wide open. Of course, we played it for all it was worth, both in and out of the ring. I basked in the blood like a crazed Roman gladiator. After sufficient bloodletting, Terry dragged me across the ring, touching all four corners, then we headed back to the dressing rooms. Before making the obligatory trip to the ER, I asked Terry: "What the hell were you doing out there, Funk? Trying to blind me?"

"That's the idea, Harley," he said with a smile. "Hey, that eye don't look so good. You oughta get it checked out."

It took 27 stitches to sew me up, but I wasn't done yet. If Funk was going to scar me for life (and he did, just look under my left eye), then I was going to get some mileage out of it. So I wore a black patch over my eye for the next several weeks everywhere I went in public, whether it was eating at a restaurant, driving or in the ring. When I went to cut promos, I wore the patch and laid into Funk. "Terry Funk, you tried to blind me in our last match," I shouted into the microphone. "But you didn't succeed. The doctors saved my eye, but no one's going to be there to save you the next time we meet."

The patch caught people's attention, and we got a spike in ticket sales for weeks. The only reason I took off the patch after a few weeks was because it caused my right eye to start becoming the dominant eye. So when I started using both eyes again, I had to put up with blurry vision and headaches until they readjusted.

(I can't claim credit for being a pioneer in exploiting real-life injuries to advance storylines. It's been done long before me, and the WWE does this more than ever these days.)

As promised, I did get Funk back for nearly sawing my eye out. But my payback wasn't actual retaliation, and it wasn't intentional. It was just another day in the ring in this crazy business. In Lubbock, Texas, Terry and I were beating each other so senseless with chairs that he left the match with a concussion and cracked vertebrae in his neck. Of course, for Terry, that's just like a stubbed toe.

By the time you read this, Terry's 60th birthday will have come and gone. But as of this writing, he's come out of retirement for the umpteenth time. A recent match involving Funk was stopped after he got wrapped up in barbed wire and passed out. "I don't remember if that was during a match or out here on the ranch," he cracked when I asked him about it.

That Texan is one tough son of a bitch, and he's got a sense of humor to boot.

The two of us probably wrestled 15-20 chain and strap matches against each other during the late '60s and throughout the 1970s. Toward the end of that run, the state athletic commissions in both Texas and Missouri stepped in and essentially told us: "Enough is enough." We had to tone down our last couple of chain matches so they wouldn't fine or shut down our respective territories.

If I wasn't pissing off athletic commissions with various wrestling antics, I was pissing off local authorities. During a match against Grizzly Smith in Amarillo our match spilled out of the auditorium into the parking lot and then into the street, stopping traffic. Finally, the police came and arrested me. I say finally, because that was our goal from the start. At the station, the cops wanted to know one thing: "Did Dory Funk Sr. put you up to this stunt?"

They had hit the nail on the head. "No, sir," I replied. "One thing just led to another, and pretty soon, we were out in the street."

I could have told Dory Sr. I didn't want to do the stunt, and he would have understood. But, like Dory, I knew the publicity would be worth it, even if it meant spending the night in the slammer.

Luckily, when I wouldn't own up to Dory's involvement, they released me. Since Dory was the promoter, they were still able to stick him with a fine. But it was a small price to pay for all the attention it got.

Years later, I almost paid a much higher price in Japan for doing the same. During the late 1970s, Abdullah the Butcher and I took it outside during a match near Tokyo. It made news across the country. Government officials were not impressed, and they threatened to put a giant red "X" on our passports. Abdullah, Baba—who by then was the owner of All Japan Pro Wrestling—

and I were required to stand before Japanese officials and explain ourselves. It was the only time I've ever seen Baba bow to anyone in my life. They eventually let us off with a public apology—and the understanding that if it happened again, we'd be banned from the country.

We were always looking for new angles or ways to shake things up for the fans. Right about the time of the previous match I described, I had another one against Funk in which we wrestled a one-fall, no-time-limit match until we started going past the auditorium's closing time. The match wasn't always action-packed, but it turned out to be the longest of my career: two hours and 11 minutes.

Terry tells a story about wrestling against me at the beginning of his career.

It was a tag-team match: Larry Hennig and me vs. Funk and Dennis Stamp. It was being filmed in Minneapolis for a TV broadcast. In the dozen minutes or so the match lasted, he says he thought he wrestled out of his mind, and was convinced he was already a great wrestler. "The next day, I went to Denver and wrestled Butch Levy and had the worst match of my life," Funk says. "I didn't realize the night before, it was Harley and Larry that made me look like a million dollars. Geez, they were putting holds on themselves. I just thought I was good. That's how dumb I was at the time."

I felt honored when Terry later told me that there was no wrestler he would have rather lost the world title to than me.

We also shared some wild times together, often heading down a Texas highway full-throttle with a case of cold beer.

On one occasion, I met up with Funk and Dusty Rhodes and his manager, Dr. Jerry Graham, in El Paso, Texas. We wrestled in El Paso that night, then had to make the drive to Odessa, Texas, for another show the next night.

The problem started when Graham decided to head across the Rio Grande for a little south-of-the-border fun that night. When he got back early the next morning, he was even drunker than usual.

That's saying something for a man who was drunk far more often than he was sober in those days. I once asked him if someone stuck a booze-filled IV into his arm before he went to bed each night. It seemed like he had a "rehab is for quitters" attitude: He went to bed drunk, woke up drunk and spent the whole day drunk.

It was this side of Graham that we saw more and more during the latter part of his career. Of course, during this period he was a shell of the man he once was.

During the 1950s and early '60s, Graham was a superstar before anyone heard of his "brother," Superstar Billy Graham. In the '50s, he teamed with Eddie Graham (real name: Eddie Gossett) to form the "Golden Grahams." Together, they headlined at Madison Square Garden numerous times, often selling every seat in the house. More than 10,000 fans were turned away from the venue when Graham challenged Bruno Sammartino for his World Wide Wrestling Federation title. He later added Superstar Billy Graham (Wayne Coleman) and Crazy Luke Graham (James Grady Johnson) into his wrestling "family."

Graham's success was in part to his colorful personality and larger-than-life aura. He pulled down huge paydays for his generation, and he spent every penny flaunting his excesses. He had new cars, suits, top hats and a shoe collection that would make Imelda Marcos envious. When it came time to cut promos, he could talk the talk with the best of them.

His gift for gab was what extended his wrestling career. Dusty Rhodes, never at a loss for words himself, could hardly get in a word edgewise when Graham was his manager. Put a microphone in his face and Graham could rip off a 20-minute stream-of-consciousness speech that sounded great until you tried to make sense of it.

The problem with Graham being drunk that night in Texas was, first, that he decided to dye his wrestling trunks a different color. Since they were the only pair of trunks he had with him, naturally he wore them into the bathtub with the dye. As Funk puts it, he apparently decided to dry off by doing somersaults around the room. By the next morning, he somehow managed to dye the bed, the carpet, the walls and everything else in the room.

And to top things off, he was still drunk to the point of being incontinent. If you don't know what that means, I'll put it to you nicely: The potty training he learned as a toddler went out the window after the umpteenth drink. Here we had a 400-pound white elephant on our hands, and Funk and Rhodes immediately stepped up with the leadership that I came to expect from them.

"He's not getting in our car," Funk said flatly, looking expectantly at me.

"You don't want me to take him…?" I asked, knowing damn well they did.

We were at an impasse. None of us wanted to take "Doc," but we all knew we needed to move him from point A to point B. That's it. Suddenly it dawned on me: We needed to move him. And what do you do when you need to move someone? You rent a U-haul, of course. So I threw Doc, his booze and a blanket into a small U-haul and we hit the road. Problem solved.

We all made it to the show that day, and Graham never once complained about his accommodations.

Doc's "brother" Eddie Gossett once told me that in Doc's heyday, while driving to a show at Madison Square Garden, he would increasingly bob his head up and down to the music on his radio. The closer he got to the tollbooth at the turnstile, the faster he would drive. As he zipped through the tollbooth, Doc would toss the proper amount of change into the chute. The vast majority of the time, he would drain it like Larry Bird shooting a three at the buzzer. It was all part of getting pumped up for the show. The good Doctor isn't with us any longer, but that's the way I prefer to remember him.

ELEVEN

FAMILY LIFE

"He came from an era of wrestling that was pretty rough. And to sit and watch your dad get the crap beat out of him on a nightly basis, sometimes I used to cry. Mom just reminded me that, 'Your dad's a tough guy; He's going to be okay.' Sure enough, at the end of the night, we were driving in a van to the next town.
—Justin Race

After winning the championship for the second time, I knew it would take a toll on my family. So we sat down and talked about how we could maintain some semblance of family life.

It wasn't easy. In my day, being a wrestler guaranteed you were on the road much of the time. If you were the champion, getting a day off was rare. We traveled so much because we took our shows to the people. We wrestled in places ranging from cow towns to bustling cities. (These days, wrestlers in the WWE typically travel and wrestle less often than we did, although their nightly audiences are much bigger on average. Plus, they have the luxury of flying more than we did through the '70s and early '80s.) Justin was nearly seven when I won the title for the second time in 1977. I was a part-time father. I didn't like it, but it was hard to avoid. Still, I wanted to spend as much time with Justin as possible during his formative years.

Our family came to an agreement: I would buy a van so that Justin and my wife at the time could be on the road with me during the summer. In 1977, I bought a Ford van and had it equipped with all the luxuries that would fit, including a TV, VCR and refrigerator. Justin brought his GI Joe and Star Wars action figures. Each summer, we would also manage to fit into the van one of Justin's cousins and a dog.

Often I would drive well past midnight until we stopped at a hotel for the night. We ate at our fair share of restaurants, but we also ate hard salami, cheese and other snacks in the van.

"To me it was just one big vacation, and Dad worked at night," Justin recently said. "But he was always up in the morning to swim with me at the hotel or visit historical Civil War areas or go to Six Flags."

Once our family was driving in a rental car in Australia. Always wanting to give Justin a taste of culture when we traveled, I asked an Aussie wrestler where we could drive to see kangaroos. He told me to head out on a certain freeway, which I ended driving up and down half the night. The next morning, I was fuming when I went and pounded on his hotel room door.

"Why the hell did you have me driving down this damn road all night?" I screamed. "All we saw was one dead kangaroo the entire time!"

He had played me. I soon realized that asking an Australian where the kangaroos are is like asking an American which highway to drive on to see the deer. He had just picked a road and had himself a good laugh.

We had our share of "Griswold family" moments. Once my family and in-laws were driving from a hotel in Georgia to pick me up at the airport. In a rush, they drove under the covered area beside the lobby, but forgot that the van had a camper shell on top. Well, the roof area beside the lobby ripped the shell right off the van, along with parts of the van roof. I ended up flying to my next destination, while they stayed and got the van repaired.

Another time we were traveling through the Civil War memorial in Vicksburg, Mississippi. At one point, we all got out to walk around, including our dog, Mitzi, a black miniature toy poodle. We piled back in and headed on our way, until, later that day when we realized Mitzi was missing.

We drove back, paid to get in the memorial again and drove through it looking for Mitzi. I wound up taking a taxi to get to my wrestling event, while the family stayed longer to look for the dog. After a fruitless search, I ended up putting an ad in the local newspaper, offering a $500 reward. That's how we got her back. But between the reward money, the cost of a flight, and the veterinarian visit required before the flight, I ended up paying about $1,500.

On a trip to Wally World—I mean Disney World—we had an experience just the opposite of the Griswolds. Instead of being greeted by an empty park, I was greeted in Magic Kingdom by an autograph seeker. Before I could sign a little boy's Mickey Mouse doll and get away, two other families recognized me and gathered around to get their Disney memorabilia signed. Before I knew it, a dozen kids and their parents were lining up for autographs as if I were making some kind of official appearance.

Justin had just got himself a pretty good sugar buzz, and he was bouncing off the walls, ready to hit the rides. So he headed off with his mother, while I stayed and signed autographs for the next three hours.

It's a good thing they didn't have that commercial back then, where someone sticks a microphone in your face and says: "Harley Race, you just won the World Heavyweight Championship. Where are you going to go?" Because Disney World would have been right near the bottom of my list of favorite places to visit, just above Somalia.

Seriously, though, it goes back to what I've always said: The fans have paid my salary since Day One, and I've always tried to go out of my way to take time for them.

The van's back seats folded into a bed so that my wife and Justin could sleep while I drove, which was usually during the night. For the next five years, this would be our routine during the summer. We went through three vans in that time, logging around 150,000 miles a year on each.

Many men push, or at least encourage, their children into their profession. Not me. My wife at the time and I actually sheltered Justin from the profession as best we could. Even when he traveled with us during the summer, we only let him watch me wrestle when we knew I was in a city that would rather carry me to the ring than lynch me in it. (Being a hated heel at the time, that could be tough.)

Often my wife would ask me whether my upcoming match was going to get ugly. If I said 'yes,' that was her cue to skip the match and take Justin sightseeing or to the movies. Sometimes we would miscalculate the violence factor, and Justin's mom would take him out of the arena as he cried.

As he got a little older, he wandered in and out of the dressing rooms backstage and pretty much knew all of the wrestlers. Once he found $240 cash on the floor and brought it to me. "It's not yours, and it's not mine, and I'm not going to ask one of these idiots whose it is," I said, motioning to the other wrestlers. So I gave the money to Vince Jr., who asked the guys if anyone lost some money.

"Is it green?" Bobby Heenan asked in a joking attempt to stake his claim to the cash.

Vince turned to give it to Justin, but I said: "It doesn't belong to him." Vince just looked at Justin and said: "No one claimed it, so it's mine. And I'm giving it to you."

As a kid, we never explained to Justin that matches are predetermined and that the other man in the ring doesn't really want to put daddy in the hospital. But we did tell him: "Don't worry,

Daddy's going to be all right." And after seeing me alive and well after each match, he became less afraid for me.

While I never wanted Justin to follow me into professional wrestling, I did encourage him to wrestle as an amateur. By the late '70s, he was on a kids' wrestling team, and doing quite well.

In 1979, he made it to the state finals in the Kansas Kids Wrestling Association. It was only his first year of wrestling. With my schedule, I knew it was damn near impossible for me to make it. But, then again, how could I miss this?

It would take a 4,000-mile whirlwind journey to pull it off.

On April 10, I said goodbye to my family and flew from Kansas City to Atlanta. A car rental took me another 67 miles to Rome, Georgia, where I defended my title against Stan Hansen that night. I headed back to Atlanta, catching a return flight to Kansas City at about 1 a.m. Two hours later, I was back in my Leewood South home. At 5:30 a.m., my family and I boarded a charter plane to Hays, Kansas.

It was there I watched Justin lose two straight matches.

Then we flew back to Kansas City, where I again parted with my family. I continued by plane another 1,227 miles to Tampa, Florida. Then I chartered a flight another 395 miles to Key West, where I whipped up on my buddy Dusty Rhodes at an event that evening. I then backtracked to Kansas City, where I collapsed into my bed.

The journey to see Justin wrestle set me back $3,200, but it was worth every penny even though he lost that time. It was the state tournament, and missing it wasn't an option.

On several occasions I went out of my way to see Justin wrestle. Once, I wrestled three times in three cities, technically on the same day: December 17, 1980. After a match in Tokyo, I flew to Los Angeles, wrestled, and then flew to San Juan, Puerto Rico, for another match. Between L.A. and San Juan, I stopped in Kansas City to see my son in a tournament.

Another time, Justin was in the state finals and I was scheduled to wrestle at the Houston Astrodome that night. I conjured up a story about the van's fan belt going through the radiator,

KING —OF-THE— RING

THE HARLEY RACE STORY

Childhood photo of me and my sister, Nadine.

Early in my wrestling career, at age 16—230 pounds.

Some of my earliest success came in Minnesota with my tag-team partner, Larry "the Axe" Hennig.

KING OF THE RING

THE HARLEY RACE STORY

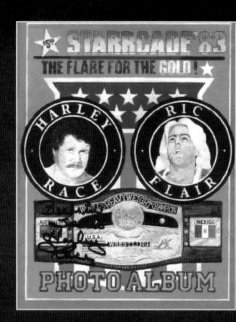

The NWA's first Starcade was headlined by a World Title match between me and Ric Flair.

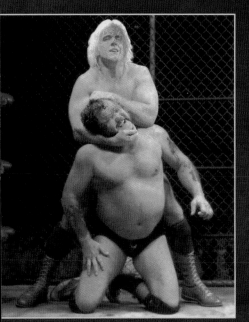

Action from the Starcade '83 Steel-Cage match between Ric Flair and me.

Ric Flair and I battled back and forth for the NWA Belt.

KING OF THE RING

THE HARLEY RACE STORY

October 6, 1978:
THE FIRST TIME ANDRE IS BODYSLAMMED!

Andre was wanting down, but I knew I was making history. Andre was seven foot two and weighed 550 pounds. I knew if I held him up long enough, someone was bound to get a picture.

Andre's Payback!

Dusty Rhodes and I had numerous title matches in the late '70s and early '80s, including the biggest match, "The Last Tango in Tampa."

KING OF THE RING

THE HARLEY RACE STORY

Meeting the Italian Stallion, Sly Stallone, in Houston, Texas.

KING OF THE RING

THE HARLEY RACE STORY

I went a step above their champion; I became "The King."

It's great to be the King!

THE HARLEY RACE STORY

The Japanese media covers wrestling much differently than their American counterparts. I got a full page in Japan.

President of pro wrestling organization NOAH, and in my opinion one of the top wrestlers in Japan, Mitsuharu Misawa.

I've made more than 70 trips to Japan, and I've always received warm welcomes.

KING OF THE RING

THE HARLEY RACE STORY

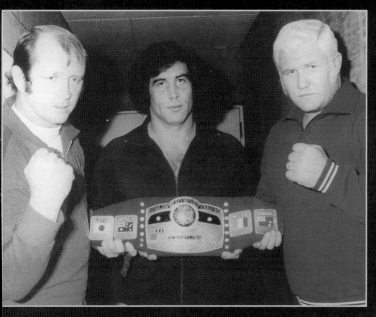

For the first time ever, three NWA world champions together in Japan, Dory Funk Jr. (left), Jack Brisco (center), and me.

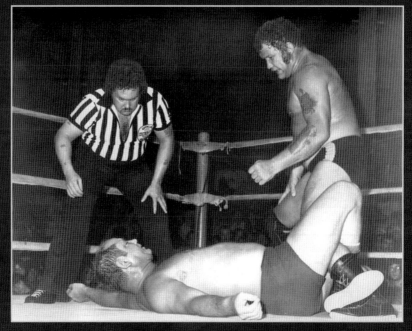

My first title reign came when I beat Dory Funk Jr.

KING OF THE RING

THE HARLEY RACE STORY

A sold-out crowd in Madison Square Garden saw a main event of Hulk Hogan and me.

The Animal knocks me on my crown!

KING —OF THE— RING

THE HARLEY RACE STORY

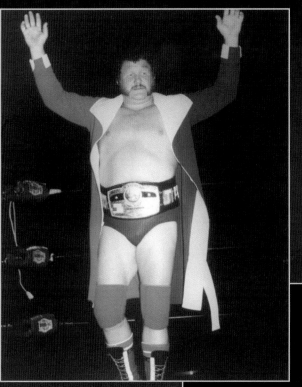

From my younger years to later years, no matter what part of the world I was in, I could always carry the title with pride and honor.

KING —OF THE— RING

THE HARLEY RACE STORY

Sam Muchnick, NWA president, exchanged the original NWA belt that had been around since the 1940s, and presented me with the new NWA belt.

KING OF THE RING

THE HARLEY RACE STORY

In Japan, I share a seat with six-time NWA heavyweight champion, Lou Thesz.

KING OF THE RING

THE HARLEY RACE STORY

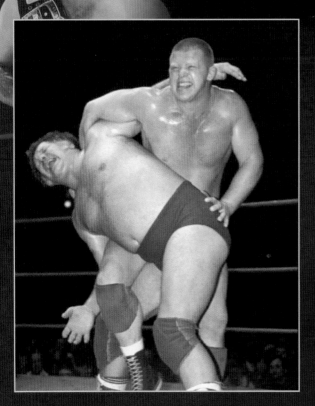

Bob Backlund and me in a title-versus-title match in Madison Square Garden, New York.

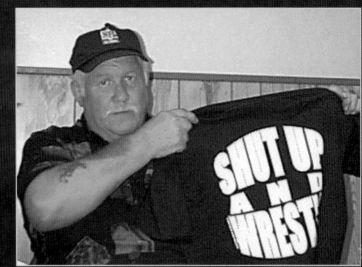

Displaying the motto of my new wrestling federation.

KING OF THE RING

THE HARLEY RACE STORY

Meeting Mr. T at Wrestlemania III at the sold-out Pontiac Silverdome (93,000-plus people).

Facing the Junkyard Dog at Wrestlemania III.

KING —OF—THE— RING

THE HARLEY RACE STORY

The woman who has made my life complete, my wife B.J.

An extended family photo. Top row, my son Rob, B.J., me, son Justin, and daughter-in-law Bobbi. Our granddaughter Miranda is between B.J. and me. In the bottom row are more grandchildren, Cierra, Grace, Luke, and Sammy.

saying there was no way I could make my show. Promoter Paul Boesch wasn't happy, and I wasn't happy that I lied to him.

That night, I watched 13-year-old Justin win the state tournament in the 14-and-under age division. He put on a dominating performance as he pinned his opponents in the 100-pound weight division.

I only missed two shows during my entire career, and both were in Houston. Incidentally, that's the same city where I lost the world heavyweight title to Jack Brisco in July 1973.

Like any family, ours also went on vacations. I loved to ski, so we often headed to the Rockies during the winter. Justin recently recounted this story:

"My uncle on my mother's side worked for John Deere and got Dad a rubberized snowmobile suit. Dad said, 'This is the best thing known to man. Why can't I take this skiing?' That was all great until he fell for the first time in this rubberized suit. He was like a 300-pound black ice cube going down the mountain on his back. He slid right through the chalet and took out a row of ski racks. Another time, he didn't know how to snowplow right and took out the ski racks again. He bent this gentleman's 14-carat gold ski polls like a horseshoe. Dad got off the ground, grabbed both of them and pulled them perfectly straight and handed them back to the guy. The guy just put his head down and walked away."

You know the type of parents who scream bloody murder at the referees during little league games? They're the ones who think that every game is for the world championship and they aren't about to let their kid lose it to lousy officiating.

Well, I wasn't that kind of dad, but there were a couple of times you might have thought differently. At any sports event Justin was in, I knew that people already would be watching me. So I made a conscious effort not to stand out. There were, however, a couple times that couldn't be helped.

Justin was playing on a tackle football team in second grade, a grade in which most schools only have flag football. But what made it dangerous was how it was regulated—or in this case, how it wasn't. Sometimes they had third- and fourth-graders playing against second-graders. On one occasion, a team of fourth-graders was pulverizing Justin's team of second-graders. To make matters worse, the referees were letting the older kids get away with penalties such as clipping and face masks. That's when I took matters into my own hands. I walked out on the field between plays and had a nice little chat with the referees. We exchanged pleasantries, and I politely informed them that, if poor officiating continued, one of these children could get injured. In my ever-so-calm demeanor, I suggested: "Perhaps we could discuss this further over some tea and crumpets sometime." Actually, now that I think about it, I might have been a little more direct—I remember them calling off the game shortly after I said my piece. Justin's team ended up forfeiting the contest, but the other parents on his team thanked me for intervening in what truly could have been a dangerous game.

On a more typical game day, I could be seen running down the sidelines with my super 8 video camera in hand, following Justin after he broke a couple tackles and was headed to the end zone.

My second intervention came during one of Justin's grade-school wrestling matches.

During a tournament, it wasn't unusual for all of the other teams to root against Justin during his matches. Not because he was a cocky kid or anything, but because they viewed him as the privileged son of a professional wrestler. I guess it was natural for them to cheer for the underdog. Justin's whole team was used to it, and they always counteracted the boos at Justin with their own cheers.

All this was fine, but during one tournament, the opposing coach went too far. I was right beside the mat watching Justin's match as he had just scored a point against his opponent by completing a reversal. Next, Justin went behind the kid to take him back down on the mat. Justin's head was directly behind the other kid's head when the kid's coach—who also happened to be his father—yelled, "Throw your head back." The kid did as he was told, throwing his head back hard into Justin's cheekbone. He ended up with a long-lasting black eye, but no serious injury.

Head-butts are an illegal move in amateur wrestling for a reason. If anyone knows the danger of head-butting, it's me. I've seen grown men babble like babies after taking them from me.

So I grabbed the coach by the shirt and practically lifted him off the ground as I said: "I heard you tell your wrestler to head-butt my son. Maybe you'd like to try to do that to me, you son of a bitch."

Fortunately for him, bystanders separated us before I had a chance to rip him a new one. It didn't take long for the cops to come, and when they did, I was arrested for assault. If I could do things over, would I handle the matter differently?

Not a chance.

TWELVE

RECORD-
BREAKING
CHAMPIONSHIP
RUN

"When he (Harley) was NWA champion, you'd always hear rumors of different stories. One rumor was that he got into a police chase in Atlanta. Wrestlers embellish everything. By the time we heard the story, they clocked Harley at 110 going around (Interstate) 285 in Atlanta...and he was pulling a boat. But that's something Harley would do."
—Bobby Heenan

G us Karras kept up a hectic work schedule through the early and mid-'70s. He could have retired earlier if he wanted. It's not like he needed the money. He just loved the wrestling business.

By the mid-1970s, diabetes was taking its toll on him. I saw Gus weekly, and it seems like every time I saw him, something else was wrong with his health. After my 1961 car wreck, Gus was responsible for convincing doctors not to amputate my leg. Unfortunately, I couldn't do the same for him. Toward the end of his life, his circulation was so poor that doctors had to amputate one of his legs. When Gus died on January 16, 1976, at the age of 73, it wasn't a surprise. Still, it hit me hard.

Nobody can replace your father, but Gus was as close to a father figure as I had. He wasn't just a good businessman—he was a good man. He gave me my start in the business, and he continued to nurture me throughout my career. He and the other partners in NWA Heart of America even had approached me about buying into the company.

Gus was as classy as they come. Most of the time I knew him, he drove a Chrysler Imperial and was one of the best-dressed men I knew. He typically wore a suit, tie, hat and a pair of shoes that probably cost as much as the rest of his outfit combined. His shoe collection would have made most women jealous—he probably owned 200 pairs. His look was completed with one of the ever-present pipes from his extensive pipe collection. In the early days, at the beginning of every wrestling show broadcast by Channel 2 out of St. Joseph, the camera would pan over to Gus and the huge cloud of smoke that he was inevitably exhaling.

Gus died a wealthy man, and through his actions he taught me why he was so successful. He truly cared about wrestling, and especially about the fans. While they waited in line to come into auditoriums, he sat outside and talked to them while smoking his pipe. It wasn't just idle chit-chat; he wanted to know what they thought of his matches and his wrestlers. He was in tune with what they liked and didn't like, and he shaped his product accordingly. I've always tried to follow Gus's lead in this respect. Even at the height of my celebrity, I've tried to remember to sign autographs and spend time talking to the fans. They're the ones who have supported me through thick and thin, and they're the ones who have paid my bills.

Gus wasn't one of the biggest promoters in the country, but you wouldn't have known that at his funeral. Everyone liked Gus, and wrestlers and promoters came from far and wide to pay their respect. Fritz Von Erich came from Dallas, Vern Gagne and

Wally Karbo from Minnesota, Sam Muchnick from St. Louis, LeRoy McGuirk from Tulsa. The list goes on.

Gus was the only person in his family in the professional wrestling business. His son went on to become a respected physician. His daughter married a man from St. Joseph, Missouri. His family sold their shares of NWA Heart of America to the remaining owners: O'Connor, Geigel and me. That made me the majority owner of the company, although O'Connor and Geigel argued that we each owned one third. In the end, it wouldn't matter. We didn't know it at the time, but the winds of change were approaching in the wrestling business. Most of the promoters, including us, would be caught flat-footed.

Just because you're the World Heavyweight Champion doesn't mean you don't have to deal with idiots. I told you about my longest match; now I'll tell you about the shortest. The year that I won the title back in 1977, *Star Wars* was all the rage. It had just hit theaters, and part of the craze was due to the robot duo: R2-D2 and C-3PO.

Like anything popular, people were finding ways to make money off someone else's product. I'm not going to stand here all high and mighty and tell you that wrestling has ever been an exception. Wrestlers have borrowed other wrestlers' moves and monikers, and storylines have been rehashed time and time again. But someone took it too far when they decided to wrestle as C-3PO.

It was my first wrestling tour in Mexico. As I slid into the ring and looked across the other side, I saw the gold-colored robot. Actually, it was a Mexican wrestler dressed in a cheesy cloth version of the robot. The whole thing screamed "trademark violation," but I guess the guy—probably correctly—figured he would fly under the tractor beam of George Lucas.

I was the champion. This was the main event. And they wanted me to wrestle a robot? So I thought to myself: "Okay, Harley, you're a professional. Swallow your pride and wrestle the stupid robot."

The bell rang. I reached out with both arms for the shoulder-to-shoulder hookup. And the robot, trying to play the part, reached out and stiff-armed me. It completely caught me off guard, and I reeled backward like an idiot. "Fine. He's done his thing. Now it's time to wrestle," I thought. So, again, I went in for the hookup. And again, the robot stiff-armed me.

The only person on this 10-day tour in Mexico who I knew for sure spoke English was the referee. So I said to the ref: "Tell that f***king moron that I'm only telling him once: Knock it off." The ref came back with his reply: "You knock it off. Work with me."

That wasn't the right answer. He had his chance to wrestle. Now it was mine. After forcing him to get me in a headlock, I took him backward in a belly-to-back suplex. But in the air, I rotated his hips, forcing him to land hard on his side. As he cringed in agony, I pinned him. They had to carry him out of the ring. Total match time: just over two minutes.

For the first time in my life, I had just violated one of the cardinal rules in our business: always watch out for your opponent's safety in the ring. It's an important rule, because we all rely on our bodies to make our living. But I knew that what I was doing would hurt him just enough to teach him a lesson. And it was a lesson that he needed to learn.

Back in the dressing room, more than a dozen angry Mexican wrestlers were standing around their man, C-3PO, making sure he was OK. As I unlaced my boots, I heard them talking and leering at me more and more.

I knew I couldn't fight 15 Mexicans. I also knew that if I put the fear of God into them, I wouldn't have to tangle with any of them. Since I liked to drink beer after wrestling, I put it in my contract for my 10-day Mexican tour that, in addition to my pay, a cold case of beer be waiting for me in the dressing room. So I picked up a bottle of beer and threw it into a mirror. The Mexicans jumped out of the way as the bottle and mirror both shattered. Then I picked up another bottle, broke the bottom of it out against the ground, and set it beside me. I then finished unlacing my boots. They stayed on their end, and I stayed on mine.

The promoter wasn't happy, and the next day he let me hear about it. "I can't have you hurting my superstars like that," he said.

I told him that his "superstars" needed to learn when to use a gimmick and when to wrestle. "I'm here to wrestle and entertain these people, not get shoved around the ring like that," I said.

The promoter didn't push the issue, and I didn't have a problem with any of the other wrestlers on the tour. And in the tradition of Mexican wrestlers, I never saw C-P3O's face.

Most of my matches as the champ weren't nearly as ugly. One of my most memorable matches early in my championship run was in 1978. I achieved something no one else had ever done, although I didn't get credit for it until years later. When Hulk Hogan body-slammed Andre the Giant at Wrestlemania III in 1986, the WWF boasted that it was the first time the Giant had been slammed. They were ignoring one small detail: I did it eight years earlier.

It was the first time I had defended my title against the big guy. I caught him perfectly coming off the ropes, ducked under him and used his momentum to lift him in the air. Normally, when you body-slam someone, you do it all in one motion. That would have been hard enough. But when I got him up, I knew there were photographers who would capture the moment. So I stopped for a second, while essentially military pressing 500 pounds. This had never been done before, so I was damn sure going to give them a chance to get the shot. As soon as the flash bulb went off, I continued the up-and-over motion to slam him. That was the risky part. It took everything I had to restart that motion and bring him through without collapsing under the weight.

The photo that was taken by a wrestling magazine photographer shows my feet sinking into the canvas as Andre covers my entire back with his two hands clasped around it.

After the match, both Andre and I convinced the photographer not to publish the photo. It's not that we didn't want the publicity. It's that Andre had a standing offer of $25,000 to anyone who could body-slam him. It was a good gimmick, and Andre didn't want to end it. So out of respect for Andre, I agreed to keep the slam as much under wraps as possible.

When Hogan repeated the feat at Wrestlemania III, the magazine published the photo to remind readers that Andre had, in fact, been slammed before.

Long before wrestling became "sports entertainment," there was a need to differentiate between the two types of wrestling: works and shoots. Nearly all matches now are works, in which the bumps and the pain is very real, but the outcome is predetermined. Shoots, on the other hand, are competitions, just like amateur wrestling. In the early 1900s, shoots were somewhat more common. Since then, they've sometimes popped up when they weren't supposed to. Once in awhile, a renegade wrestler will try to pin the wrestler who's supposed to win. It doesn't happen often, because anyone who does it won't be working in the business long.

One qualification the NWA looked for in a champion was the ability to defend his title, if a match turned into a shoot. During my career, I never once faced an opponent who tried to turn our match into a shoot.

The only "shoots" I had happened outside the ring, with one exception. This shoot happened after a match, but inside the ring.

It was after a match in Eugene, Oregon, in 1982 or 1983. About half a dozen guys who looked like stereotypical Hells Angels came to watch the show. Only they weren't satisfied watching. They were decked out in their leather and chains and they were playing up their "tough guy" images to the max. Throughout the event, they were hassling the wrestlers, "Why won't you wrestle me?" they jeered. When a wrestler took a bump and sold it, they'd yell, "That wouldn't hurt me."

As the world's champion, I wrestled last. After winning my match against Dutch Savage, I got out of the ring, and mouthed back to the bikers: "If you think you can wrestle, let's see you get in the ring." A couple minutes later, Elton Owen, the promoter, came into the locker room and told us, "Those guys are out there and they won't leave. They want to wrestle someone."

Matt Borne, a talented collegiate wrestler who would later find success as Doink the Clown, volunteered. So we went back outside and watched as Borne took on several of them, one after the other. With each one, Borne showed that he was in command, but he never hurt any of them.

The only problem was, Borne was taking it easy on the bikers, and their attitudes weren't becoming any more respectful. Finally, I said, "Come on, Matt, just hurt one of these guys and get it over with so we can all go home."

One of the bikers overheard me and looked in my direction: "Maybe you'd like to try?"

The guy looked to be the biggest and meanest of the bunch, which is exactly what I wanted. I didn't want to work my way up the ladder, having to prove myself to each of these idiots. So I warned him: "When you get in the ring with me, this isn't going to be child's play like you just saw. You'll most likely end up getting hurt."

"Bring it on," he shot back. "You're the one I wanted to wrestle to start with."

In the ring, I lifted my hands in a wrestling stance, and he put up his. He quickly lunged into me, and I flung my head full force at his. My forehead against his nose was like concrete against an egg. His nose cracked, and blood spewed out of his nostrils. Just to add an exclamation point, I cross-faced him into a version of a sleeper hold so his buddies could watch him pass out while they saw a crimson highway of blood flowing from his nose to the mat. After a couple seconds, his body went limp and I released the grip.

The gravity of the situation started sinking in when Owens immediately screamed: "Harley, you killed him! You're going to get us sued!" In reality, his injuries didn't amount to much more than a broken nose, but we didn't know that until his friends gathered around the ring and tended to his injuries.

None of his friends wanted to be the next one to step in the ring, and none of them said a word to me. In fact, nothing ever came of the incident. He got his ass kicked, and he took it like a man.

Although I've never had a match that turned into a shoot, one match did come close. Early in my championship run, I was double-crossed by a wrestler named Don Slatton. His wrestling character was "The Lawman," which was appropriate because he was a former deputy sheriff.

Slatton was a well-known practical joker. He and Terry Funk once conned Jack Brisco into wrestling in Abilene, Texas, by telling him that Texas Gov. Dolph Briscoe was related to him and wanted to meet him. Brisco agreed. He was honored, and he knew it would be good publicity to meet the governor. Funk and Slatton then arranged for Brisco to meet a friend of Slatton's who posed as the governor. They even filmed the encounter for laughs. Plus, they used Brisco's appearance to sell out the show.

The next time I saw Brisco was six months later, and I was amazed to find out that no one had told him that he was the victim of an elaborate prank. He was a tough son of a gun, so most people were probably afraid to tell him. Meanwhile, for the past half-year, Jack had been telling people about how he hit it off with the Texas governor and that they had their pictures taken together. So I told him myself.

"Jack, I don't want to have to tell you this (I did, of course. I couldn't wait to see the reaction on his face), but Funk and Slatton were jerking you around. That wasn't the governor."

Brisco didn't even believe me at first, but when he finally did, I'm not sure if he was more embarrassed or angry. His face got as red as a fire truck and he just looked at the ground and shook his head.

What Slatton tried to pull with me went beyond any kind of a joke.

Slatton and I were wrestling a chain match in Abilene, Texas. At one point in the match, we were outside the ring when Slatton gave me a good bump, then started dragging me from one corner to the next. As he headed toward the fourth, I hit him, assuming he would fall right to the floor. Instead, he stumbled forward and reached for the fourth corner, touching it as he fell.

Of course, I was the champ, and there was to be no title change that night. Whatever happened, I was determined that there wouldn't be a change. I didn't care whether the bastard did touch all four corners.

The referee was my friend Haku, and he wasn't in on the shenanigans, so he didn't call the match.

When I saw what Slatton did, I hit him with a flurry of slaps and punches, then tossed his sorry ass back in the ring. Within a few short seconds, I dragged him to each corner and Haku rang the bell.

Slatton uncuffed himself from the chain and headed for safety in his dressing room. My dressing room was on the other side of the building, so he never suspected I would come after him. I barely stayed in the ring long enough for Haku to raise my arm in victory before I dragged the 10-foot chain as I walked through the crowd and into his dressing room. Just before I entered it, I heard him and Funk talking and laughing inside.

I burst through the door and began whipping the chain around and hitting everything in my path: the lockers, chairs, pretty much anything in my way. Slatton dropped onto the floor and curled up in a ball as I stood over him with the chain in my hand.

"Please, Harley, don't hit me! Don't hit me! I'm sorry! I'm sorry," he screamed.

Of course, Terry being Terry, he quickly denied knowledge of any planned doublecross. Then he turned on Slatton, reprimanding him for trying to take the belt. Of course, Terry was probably behind it from the beginning. What would be better for business than having someone in your own neck of the woods win the belt?

Slatton lied through his teeth, claiming it was an accident. After screaming a stream of profanities at Slatton and kicking him a couple times, I let the poor bastard go.

The next time I wrestled in the Amarillo territory, I paid Slatton another dressing-room visit. After that last match between us, he had himself a belt made that proclaimed him the "world champion of the chain match." Essentially, he was saying he was the real winner of our last match. So I walked into his dressing room to retrieve his bogus belt.

He pleaded with me not to take it, telling me that it cost him good money to have it made.

"There's no earthly reason for you to have this, and I'm not leaving here without it," I told him. I grabbed it and walked out. To this day, I don't remember what I did with the stupid belt. I just know Slatton never got it back.

As wrestlers, we have to be both exceptional athletes and, at the same time, showmen. Many nights in the ring, I was all business. But even as a heel, I liked having some good-hearted fun in the ring once in awhile.

I was wrestling Ted "The Million-Dollar Man" DiBiase in the late 1970s. At the beginning of the match I noticed that he forgot to tie the drawstring on his trunks. Time to teach him a little lighthearted lesson, I thought to myself. As the heel, I was calling the shots in the ring. While Teddy had me in a headlock, I called for a "high spot"—a dazzling maneuver intended to get the audience's attention. Teddy started a sequence in which, in this case, he bounced off the ropes and hit me with a tackle, then bounced off the ropes on the other side and missed me as I ducked down. His third bounce off the ropes ended in a sunset flip, in which he bent over and I dove over him, pulling him down onto the mat in position for the pin. Everything went as planned, except that when I grabbed hold of him off the sunset flip, I latched onto his trunks and pulled them down to his knees. He was bent over mooning the audience, with everything flapping in the breeze. The audience burst into laughter while a red-faced DiBiase yanked his trunks back up. "Kid, never forget to tie your drawstring," I whispered with a smile.

THIRTEEN

A POSITION OF POWER

"Harley's not somebody who's probably lost too many fights. He's respected as being hard-nosed and tough. But if you know him, he's always a tender-hearted guy. In 1969, he ran up in that ring when nobody else did anything, and tried to save my father's life."
—Ted DiBiase

I've always tried to throw around my weight in the ring more than throwing around my influence outside the ring. Even during the height of my career, I never took political stands, took up causes to save the world, or thought about using my fame to launch another career. If people like Jesse Ventura or The Rock want to use professional wrestling as a springboard for other careers, that's great. More power to them. But I'm a wrestler, and I'm proud to say that has always been my one and only profession.

Being the world champion puts you in a position of power like no other. I have, on occasion, used my influence to help out a good friend here and there or put a smile on the face of a dying child.

You meet few people in your life who truly enrich your own life as a result of knowing them. Shohei Baba was one such person in my life. On September 4, 1980, my friendship with him surpassed even my allegiance to my employer, the NWA.

Rikidozan's Japan Pro Wrestling had split off into two groups: Antonio Inoki's New Japan Pro Wrestling and Baba's All Japan Pro Wrestling. Baba and Inoki were in a hard-fought battle to control wrestling in Japan. Baba already had the edge in profits and name recognition. He was a two-time NWA world champion, winning the belt on December 2, 1974, from Jack Brisco and then on October 31, 1979, from me. His last run as titleholder lasted two weeks before I won it back.

Now, a year later, I was on tour in Japan and wanted to do whatever I could to help my friend keep his operation the No. 1 wrestling organization in Japan.

In a secluded Japanese steakhouse, I said to Baba: "How would you like to take the belt from me?" Baba and I were scheduled to wrestle the next night.

"You're kidding?" Baba responded.

Of course, he knew I had to be joking, since the NWA hadn't scheduled a title change during this trip to Japan. An unscheduled belt switch was taboo. It was like throwing the World Series: You just didn't do it. And if you did, you had better have a damn good reason for letting your opponent pin you. Being decapitated by a vicious clothesline might be acceptable, for instance.

"No, I'm not kidding," I responded with just a trace of a mischievous smile. At this point, Baba knew I was serious, and that I was offering him a rare favor. He wasn't about to turn it down.

It actually was a clothesline that Baba used for his finishing move on me. His huge outstretched arm caught me right along my neck, stopping my upper body like hitting a wall, while my feet kept flying forward until they were parallel with the rest of my body in the air. Then my entire 260-pound frame came crashing to the mat. Baba covered me for the three-count and the Saga, Japan, crowd went nuts.

Word didn't take long to get to the U.S., and NWA officials were predictably less than enthusiastic. But they weren't there, and they had no idea what happened. Did Harley really get knocked out by Baba's clothesline, or was he granting Baba a quick title change as a favor to an old friend? I think they suspected the latter. Of course, when they asked me, I told them the former was true.

I won the belt back from Baba six days later in Otsu, Japan. But the controversy wasn't over. Back in the United States, Inoki showed up at the next annual NWA meeting in Las Vegas with a tape of the match in which Baba won the title from me.

It was Inoki's attempt to discredit both of us while getting his foot in the door of the NWA. Baba already was a member of the NWA, and that affiliation helped his business in Japan. Inoki, on the other hand, had repeatedly applied for NWA membership. He had the backing of Los Angeles promoter Mike LaBell and Vince McMahon Sr., but he still failed each time by the slimmest of margins. Baba's outfit was granted NWA membership because he applied first. The NWA didn't grant Inoki's group membership because it only wanted to be affiliated with one group from Japan.

So Inoki showed his tape at the convention, probably in hopes of replacing Baba's group as Japan's NWA affiliate. But by the time Inoki played the tape, the match was pretty much old news. The bitter feelings of NWA members who suspected I purposefully gave Baba the title were mostly fading. The reaction of most NWA members to the tape was laughter, because they could tell I did it in a way that you couldn't tell for sure what happened.

The message NWA officials gave me was basically, "The results of the tape are inconclusive, so we're not going to take any action. But don't ever let it happen again."

Meanwhile, the reputation of Baba and his All Japan Pro Wrestling soared, and his company remained the top wrestling outfit in Japan.

Slipping into the role of a mentor and teacher came naturally for me. After all, part of my job since I started working as a booker in 1970 was to keep an eye out for good talent and to help develop it.

One of the talents I was proud to help further earlier in my career was Ted "The Million-Dollar Man" DiBiase.

When his father, "Iron" Mike DiBiase, died in my arms in the ring on July 2, 1969, Ted was 15 years old. I told him the story of what happened to his father and how I tried to save his life, and ever since then there's been a bond between us.

When Ted decided he wanted to enter professional wrestling in 1975, I tried to encourage and support him the best I could. Every time I came through his neck of the woods in Texas, I made sure to take him with me when we traveled from town to town. Like me, Ted had an appreciation for fast cars. He knew that if he rode with me, we'd have a stimulating conversation while heading down the highway at 90 mph.

It was on one of those tours in Texas that I made a pledge to him: "Teddy, you've got the talent to become the world champion, and I'm going to do everything I can to help you get the belt."

During the late 1970s, Ted started working in the St. Louis territory after seeing that it was one of the country's premier territories. It was attracting top talent from throughout the nation. Ted was working his way up the ropes and putting himself in a position to become a star.

His first really big match was in 1979 at the Kiel Auditorium in St. Louis. His opponent: yours truly. I was the world champion at the time, and the seats were packed. During that match, I did everything I could to make Ted look like the star he deserved to be. That is, until I beat him. But the audience left knowing that Ted DiBiase could hold his own against the world champ.

Ted never forgot the match. "Harley was the ring general," Ted says. "He could make you look as good or bad as he wanted in the ring. He put me over big time during that match, and established me as a verified star."

It was shortly after that match that the WWF picked up DiBiase. He met Virgil, who became his valet, and started his "million-dollar man" character that would catapault him into stardom during the 1980s and 1990s.

That fame was a blessing and a curse. During the 1990s, his wife jolted him back to reality, making him realize that his worldly pursuits weren't what life was about. Ted turned over his life to Jesus Christ. He started a ministry that keeps him traveling across the nation, spreading the Good Word of the Gospel.

It wasn't just other wrestlers who I used my position to help. Starting in 1973, I used my growing fame to cheer up sick children. Shortly after becoming World Heavyweight Champion for the first time, I started visiting kids in Children's Mercy Hospital in Kansas City.

It's the kind of volunteer act that's both rewarding and depressing at the same time. It's always great to be able to make a kid's dream come true just by stopping by his hospital bed to see him. But it also depressed me at times, and it tested my faith in God. I couldn't help but wonder how such a good God can let such horrible things happen to innocent children. But everything has a purpose in His plan, and I'll never forget His plan for one child I visited.

A boy named Kevin Shatswell, who was maybe three years old, got under the kitchen sink and drank a bottle of Drano. By the time I saw him in his hospital bed, he had already undergone probably a half-dozen surgeries just to keep him alive.

He was so excited when I walked into his room that he began coughing phlegm out of a huge hole in his throat. I talked to him for a while and put a smile on his face, but when I left I knew there was no way he was going to survive.

About 26 years later—I believe it was the year 2000—I got a call from someone who asked if I remember that little boy in the hospital. "My God, yes," I said.

"That was me," the man on the other line said.

It had taken over 60 surgeries to keep him alive and repair the damage done to his body, but he was now enjoying a normal life.

Kevin was married with two children and worked for the parks department in Springfield, Missouri.

Not long after I spoke with him by phone, I put on a wrestling event near Springfield and we met each other again. We've remained friends since, and he even convinced his parks department to sponsor a couple of my wrestling events in Springfield.

FOURTEEN

DARK DAYS FOR
THE NWA

"Harley's a highly respected man in the industry: a real man. One of the toughest guys in the industry. He's got very powerful hands, but he could treat you like an egg in the ring and not break you. He had to take the most bumps, he had to drive cars the fastest, and he was always the best at what he did."
—Bobby Heenan

Right from the start, wrestling and television were a perfect match. When television came in the 1950s, station managers loved wrestling, because it provided cheap programming needed to fill time slots. Wrestling promoters loved television because it was essentially free advertising. An evolution of that relationship followed until the 1980s, which would see a revolution. Cable television was becoming commonplace, and it was about to be used by one man to wage war on wrestling promoters nationwide. Virtually everyone in the wrestling business was blissfully unaware of the looming battle. It would be over almost before the losers knew it started. By the middle of the decade, Vince McMahon Jr. would have a stranglehold on wrestling's dominant organization—the NWA.

Capitol Wrestling was the strongest territory in the nation. It covered the eastern seaboard from Virginia up to Maine and west to the Alleghenies. Its owner, Vincent McMahon Sr., had barred his son from entering the business, but finally relented in 1971. In 1973, Capitol Wrestling changed to the World Wide Wrestling Federation (WWWF). By the 1980s, the company name was shortened to the World Wrestling Federation (WWF). The elder McMahon's territory was making more money than ever, and he thought the business had reached its potential. He was looking to get out of the business, and his son eagerly snapped it up in 1982. Vince would later say that his dad would never have sold him the business if his father knew his intentions—taking it nationwide.

The first noticeable effects of the new WWF were on cable television. Vince started All-American Wrestling on the USA network. For the show, he not only hired wrestlers in his territory, but from across the United States. At first, promoters across the nation didn't mind that their wrestlers were appearing on his show. The exposure of their wrestlers could only help their business, they reasoned. What they didn't know was that cable TV was Vince's air war, and that it would be followed by a ground war that would blaze a path over territories across the nation. The troops for the ground support would be the territories' own wrestlers, who Vince started luring away. 1

As the NWA heavyweight champion, I had a unique vantage point. I was constantly traveling across the country, and I could see that Vince wasn't targeting any certain territory—he was targeting them all. I tried to impress this upon NWA president Bob Geigel. "This isn't a shot at the Midwest, Bob. This is a bull's-eye shot at the National Wrestling Alliance."

One of the first shots fired by the WWF was at the city where the NWA headquarters resided: St. Louis.

In the Gateway City, Wrestling at the Chase was synonymous with wrestling itself. The hour-long TV program started in 1962 and broadcast on KPLR Channel 11 every Saturday night.

The Koppler family owned KPLR, and Teddy Koppler Jr. knew Vince Jr. through a partnership in another business venture. Vince used his connection to convince the family to take Wrestling at the Chase off the air and let him create a new wrestling show to fill the time slot.

At the NWA, we responded by putting our wrestling show on Channel 33 in St. Louis. It had a wider reach around the perimeter of St. Louis, but it wasn't Wrestling at the Chase. By taking out our established TV show, the WWF was able to take over our market.

Another tactic Vince Jr. tried to use was to get "no-compete" contracts with the venues we had used for decades to run our shows. It meant stipulating in contracts that auditoriums couldn't have a competing wrestling show for a certain time—usually 30 days—after theirs. In Kansas City, that meant places like Kemper Arena, Municipal Auditorium and Memorial Hall. We tried to use the same tactic to keep Vince out of our territories. But it wasn't successful for either side, since federal antitrust laws prevented anyone from contracts exclusive enough to damage a competitor.

By the time the NWA territories came to a full realization of what was happening, the war was already well under way. NWA promoters held meetings across the country to brainstorm ways to defend their territories from the WWF invasion. In Chicago, we had a meeting that was attended by Eddie Einhorn, who had bought into part-ownership of the Chicago White Sox in 1980. Some ideas at the meeting involved everyone backing Einhorn or a single promoter, who would take the lead in getting the NWA national TV exposure. The problem with that, however, was that none of the promoters were willing to give that much power to any of their peers. They feared that anyone who was powerful enough to carry the torch for the NWA would be powerful enough to trample them like Vince was doing.

Promoter Jim Crockett was trying to take the lead in the NWA's fight against Vince. But many other NWA promoters saw Crockett not as our defender, but as another monopolist who wanted to win the war not for us, but for him.

The war over wrestling was more of a sneak attack than a chess match, but some NWA officials tried in vain to come up with a plan of attack. Some promoters called the senior McMahon to complain that his son was destroying their business. But by that time, McMahon Sr. was in no position to do anything about it—he was still active in the company, but by now he answered to his son.

By 1983, just one short year after Vince Jr. bought the WWF from his father, it was becoming evident that Vince Jr.'s march across the country wasn't stopping anytime soon. Vince was stealing the top talent from every territory he could. He already had stars such as Jimmy "Superfly" Snuka, Andre the Giant, "Rowdy" Roddy Piper, the Junkyard Dog and Jack and Jerry Brisco. Vince Jr. stole Billy Jack Haynes out of Don Owens' Portland territory. By the end of the year, Vince's coup d'etat would be the acquisition of a wrestler who had just risen to fame as "Thunderlips" in *Rocky III*: Hulk Hogan.

Another problem the NWA territories had in their fight with the WWF was money. It's not that territory owners didn't have money to wage the war—they just didn't want to invest their life savings to wage a war that might not be winnable.

Money, however, wasn't the main reason the territories weren't willing to wage a full-scale war. The main factor was their age. Many of the owners were nearing retirement age and weren't driven by the hunger that so often accompanies youth. They had already made their money; now they just wanted to lock in what profits they had remaining before even that was too late. It's not that they didn't care or have any fight left in them, but it wasn't enough, and it wasn't unified.

Still, the NWA was planning a new event that it hoped would be large enough to drive back Vince's forces and keep the NWA on firm footing. I would put my World Heavyweight Title on the line against Ric Flair on November 24, 1983, in Greensboro, North Carolina. The coliseum held 17,000 people. It would be piped into half a dozen other venues across the country via closed-circuit TV—the first time it had been used for a straight wrestling match. (Closed-circuit TV, a forerunner to pay-per-view, was first used in a match in the 1970s between boxer Muhammad Ali and wrestler Antonio Inoki. By the time the bore-fest was over, people wanted their money back.)

I agreed to the event, which was heavily promoted through other televised events throughout the country.

Two days before the event was to take place, Vince Jr. called to ask if he could fly me to Connecticut to meet him. He didn't say why, and he didn't need to. I didn't have anything to lose by listening to what he had to say, so I agreed. Vince flew my wife and me to Greenwich, Connecticut. The meeting was held at an upscale restaurant there. In attendance were Vince, Jim Barnett, myself, and our wives. After we ate, Vince cut to the chase.

"Harley, you know why I asked you to come here. I want you to wrestle for the WWF."

He made me a $250,000 offer to jump ship. It wasn't the kind of offer that you took to your attorney and mulled it over with your family for a few days. He wanted an answer, and he wanted it before he picked up the bill.

The need for speed was part of Vince's master plan. Vince already had hired away many of the top wrestlers in the country. But in order to rip the heart out of the NWA, he wanted to lure away its World Heavyweight Champion. He wanted me to back out of Starrcade and take the belt to the WWF, presumably where they would have me face the WWF champion in a "title unification" bout.

The offer was tempting. I had $500,000 invested in Heart of America Wrestling, and I was in the process of losing my investment. It was a chance to go from losing money to making money.

But for how long? At the time, Vince was succeeding in taking his product nationwide. But it wasn't a sure thing. Others had tried and failed. In the 1960s, for example, Vern Gagne tried to muscle his way into Minnesota and California. The NWA banded together to fight the move, and the top wrestlers in the country did stints in Los Angeles for promoter Mike LaBell as a way to keep Gagne out of the territory.

I excused myself to go to the bathroom, and, after a couple minutes, he followed.

We stood in front of a full-length mirror, which I pointed to. "Vince, what do you see?" I asked.

"You and me in that stupid mirror," he shot back.

"Yeah," I said, motioning to the mirror. "And I've got to look at that person when I wake up tomorrow."

"Then evidently you've answered my question," Vince said, and then proceeded to turn around and walk out.

I wasn't the only person to underestimate Vince's ability to take over. Promoters across the country didn't see the threat until it was practically too late. The main reason, however, that I turned Vince down was because it would mean double-crossing the organization that had paid my bills from Day One. I also would have admitted defeat, something I'm not accustomed to.

You're only born with so much pride. Each time you do something to dishonor who you are and what you believe in, you lose some of it, and eventually you become an empty shell. My pride wouldn't let me take Vince's offer. Not after I had already pledged to lose the NWA title at Starrcade.

It was an emotional decision, and one I'd have to live with for a long time. Was it the right decision? As a business decision, probably not. But from a moral standpoint in a business where your word means everything, it was the only honorable thing to do.

Vince never raised his voice, but I could tell he wasn't happy with my answer. He wasn't accustomed to being turned down. As we walked out of the restaurant, the cordial nature of our meeting took a turn for the worse. It's hard to imagine a dinner meeting turning violent. But this is, after all, the wrestling business.

Vince and his wife were walking a few steps ahead of the rest of us, when I saw Vince start to walk with more of a swagger. Without saying a word, he pivoted his foot and swung around to face me, then dove at my legs in an attempt to take me down. Barnett acted instinctively by shrieking and jumping out of the way. I acted instinctively by cross-facing Vince with my left arm, getting his head in a position where breaking his neck would be easy. I was angry enough to do it. In the split second I had to decide what to do next, my wife grabbed my head and said, "No, don't do this." I released my grip and let him go.

That night I kept my loyalty to the NWA and kept my pride. But I would later realize that, with or without me, Vince's WWF was going to replace the longstanding system of territories just like Wal-Mart replaced many mom and pop stores across the nation.

Later, Vince said that despite putting on a strong front while expanding nationwide, his operation was more exposed than people realized.

"We did it all with mirrors, it was all cash flow. Had those promoters known that I didn't have any money, they could have killed us," he said.[2]

While this incident makes for a good story, it is an isolated incident that shows our relationship at its most strained point. Time would heal our wounds over the years, and I would come to count Vince as a friend.

---

[1] Some background information on the WWF going nationwide was taken from *The Complete Idiot's Guide to Pro Wrestling*, Second Edition and *Pro Wrestling: From Carnivals to Cable TV.*

[2] *The Complete Idiot's Guide to Pro Wrestling*, Second Edition.

FIFTEEN

PASSING THE TORCH

"Dad was adamant when I was a kid that if someone asked you for an autograph, you do it. They pay your salary. He said I should follow suit if someone asks me for my autograph. I've given my autograph out thousands of times, though I'm not sure why. There would be people who you wouldn't think Harley Race would give the time of day to, and Dad was speaking to them for five or ten minutes. It would make their entire week."

—Justin Race

Back around the late '70s and early '80s it seemed like I was wrestling Dusty Rhodes in my dreams when I wasn't wrestling him in person. I've probably had as many matches with him as I have with anyone.

One of the most memorable matches we had together was the "Last Tango in Tampa," a show in 1980 that Dusty produced. It was the first huge outdoor wrestling show in the South.

Dusty built up the match by promising to retire if he didn't beat me, and 35,000 people showed up to watch.

Dusty's always been a big guy, but his size was deceiving because he was always in better shape than his body would lead you to believe. He kept up with me move for move for a full 60 minutes. In fact, Dusty kept up with me better than the referee, NWA President Fritz Von Erich. He got so tired of getting down on the canvas and counting to two that he ended up staying down on one knee. I guess he figured we'd be back down there soon enough, so it wasn't worth standing up.

I won the match with two of three falls, but Dusty claimed the one time he pinned me (he got me with his Bionic Elbow) gave him the out he needed so he didn't have to retire.

That match was one of the best we ever had together, if not the best.

Since it wouldn't have been acceptable for me to hang out with "The American Dream" outside the ring, the few words we spoke to each other were mostly inside the squared circle. Dusty still recalls when he walked into the ring to face me in St. Petersburg, Florida, in 1976, and my reaction upon seeing that he had a string in his ear. He had just pierced his ear, and was using the string to keep the hole open until he could put an earring in it.

"I wanted to do it to piss everybody off, and to piss Harley off," Dusty said. "Back in 1976, it wasn't fashionable for a man to wear earrings. Harley was a man's man. We walked to the center of the ring to get the instructions, and Harley says to me: 'What kind of a f★★★king man would wear a f★★★ing earring?!' I just wanted to crawl under the table."

Dusty could dish it out, too. He'd often mock my yellow and black robe, calling it a "Hertz rent-a-car robe," because he said it looked just like one in a Hertz commercial.

I had gladly given up the title to Dusty in 1981, but by 1983 I wanted it back. Only this time, it was more about business than my competitive drive.

The WWF wasn't wasting any time in its battle for wrestling supremacy. At Heart of America, like other territories, the WWF was hitting us hard in the pocketbooks. I knew that the best way to reverse the trend, at least temporarily, was to get back the belt. Call it short-sighted or self-centered if you like, but I knew that being the champ would give a boost to our operations in both Kansas City and St. Louis.

Getting the needed votes from the Championship Selection Committee wasn't as easy this time. I had been the champion six times previously, and there was a growing sentiment to use the belt's influence to build up another generation of stars, including wrestlers like Barry Windham, Dick Murdock, and Ricky Steamboat.

The Puerto Rico territory stepped in to cast the vote I needed to give me the title. Many of the boys avoided the territory because it was a dangerous place. If you didn't watch your back, you could easily get stabbed or shot at by unruly fans. They even put up plexiglass around their rings for the wrestlers' safety. I think the territory's owners appreciated the fact that throughout my career, I never shied away from wrestling in their territory.

I took the belt for the seventh time from Flair on June 10, 1983. Like I had hoped, the five-month run gave a boost to both me personally and to our Heart of America territory. One tactic I used to combat the WWF was to start challenging their champion, Bob Backlund, to a match. Every territory I wrestled in, I emphasized that I was *the* world champion, and that until their so-called champion won the belt from me, he wasn't a true champion.

In retrospect, it was like patching a collapsing dam. My seventh title run put some money in my pockets, but the WWF still seemed unstoppable.

Late in the summer, Jim Crockett started to organize and finance the initial Starrcade event, which would be a cage match in Greensboro, N.C. Crockett ran the Mid-Atlantic territory and was one of the top promoters.

Flair and I had wrestled countless times before. We needed a good gimmick to sell the match in multiple cities. Crockett came up with a good one: In an attempt to avoid wrestling Flair and putting my title on the line, I would put a bounty on Flair's head.

"I didn't think that there was anything on the face of the earth that would ever push me to do what I'm gonna do right now!" I barked into the microphone while taping a promo. "But Flair, (you've pushed) me as far as you're going to push."

"Right here is $25,000, and it goes to any human being that can eliminate Ric Flair from wrestling. ...I'll give it to any living human being. It's here for you. Come and get it, please. Somebody take the damn money! I want rid of Flair!"

Of course, the inherent risk with essentially putting a "hit" on Flair was that a wrestling fan would take it seriously, and might attempt to—at the very least—injure Flair to collect the cash. Crockett and I hashed out the concern, and in subsequent promos I changed my offer from "any human being" to "any wrestler."

The storyline culminated during a tune-up match between Flair and me. As Flair applied his trademark figure-four leglock on me, Bob Orton Jr. charged into the ring and leaped off the ropes, landing on the defenseless Flair. Dick Slater—dressed in an open shirt, blue jeans and cowboy boots—then joined Orton in stomping on Flair as he lay helpless on his back. Orton proceeded to pile-drive Flair, then grab his head and snap it to one side in an apparent neck-breaking move. Meanwhile, Slater high-fived me as I pointed to Flair's limp body and laughed. The three of us left the ring, and "Rowdy" Roddy Piper and other friends of Flair ran to his aid before medical personnel hauled him off on a stretcher.

Crockett and a cameraman followed me back in the dressing room, where I gleefully handed out the $25,000 bounty to Orton and Slater.

"Harley Race, you're the worst excuse for a champion I've ever seen," Crockett spouted. "I don't care what you think, Crockett," I growled. "It's done! Take a look at the cash!"

Flair furthered the storyline by cutting a promo in a neck brace, telling the fans: "At one time I thought there was nothing I wanted in the whole world more than a heavyweight championship. Now I'm not sure." He went on to thank his fans for their support, and then announced his retirement from wrestling.

But before long, Flair was back. Wielding a baseball bat and still wearing a neck brace, Flair chased Orton and Slater out of the ring while they were wrestling in a tag-team match. Flair then screamed an out-of-retirement diatribe into the microphone.

"It'll be a cold day in hell when someone can walk out here and make fun of me, put me in the hospital, try to break my neck, try to end my career," he yelled, his face growing redder with each sentence. "And Race, I promise you, Race, for paying those guys $25,000, before it's all over, I'll have a piece of you. And it's gonna be the gold belt!"

I responded by expressing displeasure that the match had been secured. Reluctantly accepting the challenge, I told Flair that what Orton and Slater did to him was nothing "compared to what I am going to do to you."

The hyping of the event was complete. Flair was the likable up-and-coming star, and he dubbed his bid for a second run at the title "A Flair for the Gold."

I, on the other hand, had the fans booing me every step of the way. I was the evil titleholder, who used all the tricks in the book to dodge a battle that could result in me giving up my coveted title.

In front of the cameras, I was the angry heel. But the real me was more depressed than angry. If I was angry at anything, it was the wrestling business.

The pressures of being the world champion most of the time since 1977 had taken its toll. I was earning $400,000 a year at my peak in the late '70s and early '80s, but I didn't have time to enjoy my money. I was on the road and away from my family the vast majority of the time. My marriage was failing. Our Heart of America territory was bleeding red from the WWF's nationwide expansion.

There was also the physical toll. In the early 1980s, I started feeling pain more often and in more parts of my body. My back had never healed from that match that caused me temporary paralysis in Amarillo in the early 1960s. Performing daily stunts such as diving head-butts wasn't helping matters.

In this business, you learn to live with pain. As your career progresses, so does the pain. With each advancing year, my body's cry for retirement became louder. But my heart always told me to keep pushing on. I worked for two decades to get to the top, and I managed to stay at the top for the better part of seven years. Where do I go from here?

I was never into the recreational drug scene, and I didn't gulp down painkillers after my shows. The limited pain management I did use typically came in a 12-ounce can, preferably just above the point of freezing. After matches and on the road, I was known to drink sometimes up to a case of beer at a time.

I was fed up with the wrestling business, and I knew my run as titleholder was coming to an end. That was mostly a good thing. I was burned out and bordering on depression.

The match itself was a cage match with a one-hour time limit. As part of the hype, I argued that it was demeaning for me as the champ to wrestle in a cage match. But Crocket told fans it was needed to ensure there would be no interference and a clear-cut winner. Cage matches often are a way of hinting to the fans that they'll likely see blood, and this one was no exception.

The match started as Flair walked out to his theme song, "2001: A Space Odessey." The arena was dark except for a few laser lights and a rotating disco-style ball hanging from the ceiling, like you'd see at "cosmo night" at the local bowling alley. The music stopped for a few seconds before an explosion and smoke accompanied Flair's entrance. (It all seemed pretty grand for 1983, but today's wrestling show pyrotechnics would put it to shame.) He entered the cage in a blue robe that sparkled with silver sequins. After a couple minutes I slowly made my way into the ring wearing a red, white and blue robe with "Race" written on the back.

Former world heavyweight champion Gene Kiniski served as the referee. Incidentally, one of the main things I remember about the match is how clumsy Kiniski was during the match. He was constantly getting in the way, almost like he thought he was supposed to be the star of the show.

After 10 minutes, it seemed like Flair was all but finished. I had executed knee and elbow drops, a neck-breaker and a diving head-butt. I had tossed Flair into the metal links and pile-driven him into the mat. Twelve minutes into the match, Flair's bleached-blond hair was rapidly turning red with blood.

Of course, it didn't take long for the tide to turn. Just a couple minutes later, my face was bloodied and Flair was in control, letting out his cocky "whooo!" before dropping a knee to my head and pile-driving me.

Nearly 20 minutes into the match, Flair applied his figure-four before I reversed it to shift the momentum again.

"Ric Flair, the challenger, ... appears now that he is certainly not going to be able to take the edge here on world heavyweight champion Harley Race," announcer Gordon Solie said. Solie was one of the best—he was known as the Walter Cronkite of wrestling. He worked his gift of gab to get over even the weakest wrestlers to audiences.

After a vertical suplex by Flair, I head-butted Kiniski, who struggled to get up while I cornered Flair. Flair fought his way out of the corner with four unanswered blows, then climbed to the top of the turnbuckle, heaving his body onto me. I fell to the floor and Flair covered me as Kiniski administered the three-count.

"Ric Flair has done it! No question about it. Ric Flair has just defeated seven-time world heavyweight champion Harley Race," Solie intoned as the audience got on their feet and cheered.

The match lasted close to 24 minutes. As far as I was concerned, it was 24 minutes in my life that I would never get back. I was tired, sore, and disgusted with the wrestling business. The entire event was just Jim Crockett's attempt to compete on a nationwide level with Vince. Meanwhile, I was the one taking the bumps in the ring and losing money out of the ring with the Heart of America territory.

The only thing I felt good about was that I was able to pass the torch to my good friend Ric Flair. It was the start of his third run as champion, and he would go on to win the belt a total of 16 times as of this writing.

In my postmatch interview, I put on my game face and told the fans that I'd be back as champion for the eighth time. Then I sent a message to Flair: "I'm not packing it up and going away (to) hide. I'm going to hound you like you've never been hounded before in your life. You drove me absolutely insane for six months. I'll guarantee you that you will live in hell until you meet me again!"

It was Thanksgiving night, but I was feeling anything but thankful. I walked into the dressing room, took off my boots, unlaced them, and tossed them into a trashcan. As far as I was concerned, I was through wrestling.

SIXTEEN

IF YOU CAN'T
BEAT 'EM ...

"Harley had a reputation of having a heavy foot on the throttle. In his own way, it was kind of a signature of his. He loved credit for covering lots of space in little time. And he was daring. Sometimes I heard of his driving before his wrestling when he first started out."
—Nick Bockwinkle

My seventh NWA World Heavyweight Championship run ended at the Starrcade match, and I felt physically and emotionally battered. When I lost the title previously, I had always had one goal in mind: getting it back. This time was different. I had won the belt seven times, and I didn't feel the pressure or the hunger to be the top dog again. I also felt free from the restraints of a breakneck schedule and the burden of carrying the torch for an entire organization. I learned long ago that when you're the champion, your life is not your own. It belonged to the NWA, and you worked damn near every day to bolster the organization in territories across the country and abroad. It was a little like being a traveling salesman. Only instead of getting a door slammed in your face, you got chairs slammed in your face.

After Starrcade, I went into a well-needed seclusion at Lake of the Ozarks. I was at peace in this beautiful spot in mid-Missouri. Even then, I knew it was where I wanted to retire. I spent my days watching television and just relaxing. A few days quickly turned into a couple months. I was enjoying the relaxation, but there was always a question in back of my mind: How are we going to be able to turn things around and save the NWA? Jim Crockett was taking the lead by getting NWA a TV slot on TBS. He was billing himself as NWA's savior, but it just looked like he was looking out for Number One.

Crockett was supposedly going to use the TBS show to make stars out of the top NWA wrestlers from across the country, but it didn't work out like that. With only one show a week, he didn't have the airtime for everyone. So he mostly gave it to the wrestlers in his own Georgia territory. Other territories suffered by first having their stars raided by Vince's WWF, then by not getting promised help from Crockett in building up the talent that remained.

Meanwhile, Crockett sent some of the NWA's top talent from Georgia to wrestle in the various territories as a way to help the territories. But the boost it gave them was offset by the financial cost of the territories to bring in the stars. Promoters had to pay top dollar, plus airfare, to bring in a big name like Flair, Barry Windham or Ricky Steamboat.

After a couple weeks relaxing at my lake home, the phone started ringing. First it was Pat O'Connor and Bob Geigle, wondering how much more time off I needed. Then they had other wrestlers, including Flair, bugging me on a daily basis, "Harley, when are you going to get your ass back here and help us out? We're in the middle of the fight of our lives with the WWF, and we can't do this without you."

I ignored their pleas for several weeks. I was burned out, and I was in no rush to return to the Kansas City office. When I eventually did, four or six weeks later, I went back to the office, but not the ring. My vacation didn't give me much of an attitude adjustment. I still faced the same problems as before: My career was on the down side, my marriage was failing, and I felt helpless against the WWF's onslaught.

My Heart of America partners encouraged me to get back in the ring. They said that if anyone could bring in the crowds to stave off the WWF, I could. Truthfully, they probably just wanted me out of the office so they wouldn't have to put up with my short temper.

But what eventually led me to lace up my boots again was money, pure and simple. Working in the office, I saw the bills pile up as our operation continued to run in the red. I had a $500,000 investment in Heart of America, not to mention other money I foolishly sank into it to keep it afloat. I needed to wrestle to recoup some of my losses. But I learned my lesson this time, and I wasn't about to throw good money after bad. The money I made from here on out was staying in my family. The NWA might have been a sinking ship, but that didn't mean I had to keep playing with the band.

I'm not about to tell you some sob story about my financial troubles. I realize I was earning in a year what it took the average person a good part of their career to bring in. But no matter how much you make, you get accustomed to your standard of living. When your salary falls, so does that standard of living. Unexpected college expenses don't help either.

By the mid '80s, my son, Justin, had graduated from high school and enrolled in Southern Methodist University in Dallas. Between football, wrestling and academic scholarships, he nearly had a full ride. Not long into his college career, however, he had an X-ray done on his neck and discovered he had injured a vertebrae while wrestling in high school. That meant an end to his college athletic career and scholarships. His academic scholarship was never in jeopardy—he carried a 4.0 grade point average. Still, college isn't cheap, so Mom and Dad stepped up to the plate to make sure he got a good education.

When I started wrestling again, I continued a tactic I previously used to wage war against the WWF. Since NWA wrestlers were defecting left and right to join the WWF, I had used my status as NWA champion to belittle the WWF and its wrestlers.

Wherever I wrestled, I challenged their champion to meet me in the ring. "The WWF can't say they have a world champion until they beat me," I growled in taped promos and in the ring. Even after I lost the belt for the last time, I would openly mock the WWF and challenge various WWF champions—including Bob Backland, the Iron Sheik and Hulk Hogan—to face me in the ring.

I took steps to let anyone who joined the WWF know that they now were considered the enemy. They were contributing to my financial losses, and I took it personally, especially when the WWF was putting on a show in my territory.

I almost went too far to make that point one night. In early 1985, the WWF held a show in Kansas City's Municipal Auditorium. I went for the sole purpose of disrupting the show and letting the WWF and its wrestlers know that they weren't welcome in my hometown. I also was going to make the point that they couldn't keep me out of Municipal Auditorium, even for one night. It was one of the venues we used for our shows. No one had previously rented it to compete with us.

I even had an office in the building, so getting inside wasn't an issue. I boldly walked into the main dressing room, and saw Terry and Dory Funk sitting down looking at me with stunned looks on their faces. Hulk Hogan was facing them, so he saw the look on their faces. Before he could turn around, I slapped him in the rib cage from behind and smirked a little while watching the startled Hulkster jump. He then lost his balance and fell backward into a chair.

It was a tense situation. Everyone knew I wasn't there for tea and biscuits. Hogan tried to break the ice: "Harley, I thought the first time I saw you in Kansas City you'd have a great big gun."

Hogan knew my reputation as a gun-lover. At one time, I owned hundreds of guns.

"I don't have a great big one…" I said as I lifted my shirt to reveal a .380-caliber handgun stuck down the front of my pants.

Hogan's attempt to defuse the tense situation had backfired, and now the pleasantries were over. Gorilla Monsoon, a road manager for the WWF at the time and one of the nicest men you'll meet in the wrestling business, stepped forward. "Harley, you have to leave the building," he said. Gorilla was one of the first people I wrestled in my career back in the early '60s, and I considered him a friend. Security had already been called, but they knew the dispute involved me and they were reluctant to get involved.

"I know I have to leave, but I'm not going to leave before I let people know I'm here," I told Gorilla. Then I started making my way toward the stage.

I was soon flanked by two of Kansas City's finest, while Gorilla continued to warn me. "Harley, I can't allow you to do this. If you go up in the ring, I'll have no choice but to have you arrested."

As I entered the auditorium walking toward the ring, the chants started: "Harley! Harley!" They knew I was in the building. I had made my point. No need to get arrested and make a scene, I figured. Besides, I didn't want to put Gorilla in the position of having to have me arrested. So as I approached ringside, I turned around and walked out.

The audience was left wondering why I made a cameo at a WWF event. But they didn't wonder for long. We used the incident to pump up our own events in the Kansas City area. At each event shortly after the incident, I would boast to the crowd that I walked into their event and confronted the WWF and its wrestlers.

In Hogan's book, his version of the story has me lighting the WWF's ring on fire. It never happened. I have no idea where he came up with that, since I walked close to the ring, but never actually got to it.

Being a jerk that night was more out of stubbornness than anything else. I was stubborn because deep in my heart I knew that fighting the WWF was a lost cause. But I was angry with the WWF, and this was my way of lashing out.

After winning and losing the belt for the eighth time, I continued to wrestle but the months seemed to drag on. Part of the reason was because I knew that my reign as champion was likely over. Plus, every month it became clearer and clearer that the face of wrestling was changing. I was at a crossroads in my life. I knew I couldn't just keep pushing on, oblivious to the change. My choices amounted to either retiring or somehow adapting in a way that would prolong my career.

In late 1985, I met with Geigle, O'Connor, Crockett and Gagne to discuss the future of the NWA. The meeting was held in the Delta Airlines Ambassador Room at Kansas City International Airport. It was a courtesy room reserved for ultra-frequent flyers like myself. Once again, we needed to come up with a plan to survive. This time, I had hoped to hear something different.

Crockett talked about how he was going to let his talent work for NWA territories across the nation, but that he needed to have a say in the match-ups and outcomes of the matches. Gagne replied by saying nobody was going to give orders in Minneapolis but him. It was what I hoped wouldn't happen, but what I mostly expected. Everyone wanted to protect their own territories and interests, but nobody had the vision or leadership to unite the NWA in a way that could return it to its former glory.

After the others had their say, I made the announcement that I suspected I would have to make. What I was about to tell them was tough, but I wanted to be man enough to tell them to their faces. "Guys, effective today, I'm done," I said. "Unlike many territory owners, I'm still at the age where I can shift gears and recover from my losses. I'm going to do what's best for my family. I'm going to join the WWF."

SEVENTEEN

KING OF THE RING

"Dad accidentally slammed my finger in the sliding van door when I was young. In the hospital, my finger was throbbing, and a nurse walked in with an eight-inch hypodermic needle. All she was doing was putting it away. But before she did, Dad said, 'That's the needle they're going to use.' That was his way of showing love—scaring the shit out of me."

—Justin Race

When I told my NWA partners I was quitting to join the WWF, I hadn't even struck a deal yet with the WWF. An employee of ours at Heart of America had previously quit for a job with the WWF. Like others who had done the same, I told him that he would be missed, but that I understood he needed to do what he felt was best for his future. Since he left, we kept in touch, and he had encouraged me to join the WWF. He had assured me the company had a spot for me if I decided to join.

Crockett and my Heart of America partners probably weren't shocked to hear me say I was quitting, but in a way they must have been taken aback to hear that I was joining the very operation that I had come to despise. I don't remember any of them speaking a word at that meeting after I made the announcement. They probably knew my mind was made up, and that they'd be wasting their breath trying to talk me out of it. After wishing them good luck with the NWA, I walked out of the meeting.

Pay negotiations between Vince and me were kept to a minimum. He basically asked me what I was averaging a year with NWA, then responded: "That sounds fair to me." My first match wasn't for a month, but Vince asked me to cancel a three-week tour in Japan that I was about to start. He paid me the $30,000 that I would have made there.

Despite being a part owner of Heart of America, there was never a discussion about selling my share of the company to my partners. There wasn't much in the way of physical assets, and the company's value had plummeted. I just wrote off my $500,000-plus investment as a total loss.

My first match under the WWF banner was in Maple Leaf Gardens in Toronto, Canada. It was the same building that I walked out of with the world heavyweight title in 1977. But when I walked in this time, all I could think of was whether I had driven the final nail into the NWA's coffin.

I'll never forget walking into that dressing room for the first time. It would have been uncomfortable enough just because the WWF guys and I had been working for competing companies. What made things even more tense was the fuel I had thrown on the fire by essentially mocking them and their organization for the past three years. Now I was joining them. I had walked into the WWF's dressing room once before as an enemy. Now I was about to walk into their dressing room as a colleague.

I entered, and the room fell silent. It was an eerie, awkward feeling for all of us. Most of the boys eventually told me they were glad to see me join the WWF. A few indicated they were relieved that I was no longer going to be a pain in the ass from afar. Some of them, I imagine, were still angry at me. They did-n't say it, but I knew what they were thinking: "Harley, you hyp-ocritical SOB. How could you accuse us of double-crossing and backstabbing the NWA all that time only to do the same thing we did?"

Still, I didn't feel like I needed to apologize to anyone, and I didn't. Most of them knew that the hard time I gave them and the WWF was just business, just like my decision to join the WWF was business. They knew not to take it too personally.

The lukewarm reaction I first got at the WWF didn't matter after a few days. Before long, I had rekindled relationships with old friends like the Funks who I had lost touch with when they went to the WWF.

The two wrestlers I first befriended at the WWF, however, were wrestlers who weren't involved in the NWA-WWF battle. Dynamite Kid (Tommy Billington) and Davey Boy Smith were cousins from England who moved to Calgary to wrestle for Stu Hart's Stampede Wrestling. The pair had jumped to the WWF, and were gaining fame as the British Bulldogs.

I had hung out with them when I traveled to Calgary each year for the Calgary Stampede. After I joined the WWF, we often drove together to shows.

These two kids worked hard and played hard, and they were always a blast to be around. Dynamite was a daring and under-rated wrestler with a full arsenal of traditional and high-flying moves. Davey Boy was also an incredible talent who in 1992 would win the Intercontinental Championship belt in the WWF in front of 80,000 fans in London's Wembley Stadium.

Both of them would later face different drug-related tragedies in their lives. Davey Boy died in 2002 at the age of 39 after suf-fering an apparent heart attack. He had battled drug addiction and been released by the WWF two years earlier. Dynamite would later face serious health problems stemming from steroid use and back injuries. By his 40th birthday, he would be practi-cally confined to a wheelchair.

In the WWF, I used my "handsome" moniker as well as the saying: "The greatest wrestler on God's green earth." But one thing you never saw was the WWF bill me as the "eight-time world champion." They wanted to promote me in their organization as one of the top wrestlers on the planet, but they understandably didn't want to recognize my NWA affiliation. (They didn't really need to, anyway. The fans already knew my credentials.) So the question came up: What can we do to promote you and give you a fresh new identity in the WWF?

I talked with Vince about possibilities, and he came up with an idea. "Harley, what's a step above champion?" he asked, then proceeded to answer his own question, "King." The term had been used by wrestlers before, including Jerry Lawler and Ernie Ladd, but no one had ever won the title in a tournament.

On July 14, 1986, the WWF staged the second "King of the Ring," a tournament held in Foxboro, Massachusetts. (Many people have since forgotten the first "King" event that was held a year earlier.) Fourteen wrestlers, including myself, competed for the title as 12,000 fans watched in Sullivan Stadium.

In the last of my three matches, I won the tournament by defeating Pedro Morales, the World Wide Wrestling Federation champion from 1971 to 1973.

Not long after that, an extravagant "coronation" ceremony was held at a wrestling event in Hartsford, Connecticut. Several midgets, including Lord Littlebrook—the only little person to be inducted into the WWE Hall of Fame—brought into the ring the robe and a purple pillow with the crown perched on top. As I sat on a throne in the middle of the ring, I was crowned and bestowed with an ornate purple robe. Some of the top wrestlers in the business came to watch.

In that tournament, my "handsome" moniker was replaced by "king" in the eyes of many of the fans. Many still know me as "King" Harley Race even today. Which moniker is my favorite? I honestly can't pick one. I've had several throughout my career, and each seemed appropriate at the time.

The King title also solidified my transformation from a hated heel to a beloved elder statesman. I never intentionally changed my image. With me, what you see is pretty much what you get. But now even the fans who paid good money to boo me in the '60s and '70s were now on my side.

Some wrestling followers have criticized the "King" title and tournament, blasting it as just a hokey gimmick designed to let the WWF have yet another titleholder. I thought it was a fitting way to promote me in the organization. Judging by the fans' reaction, I think they agreed. I never viewed the King title as an equivalent to the world heavyweight title, but I tried to treat it like it was.

I was on the down side of my career and physically past my prime. But when I wore that crown and robe into the ring to defend my title, I brought my "A" game. I wrestled with a renewed vigor that fans hadn't seen in years. The title not only boosted my name, but it helped me raise the bar as far as my wrestling.

One of the downsides of being king was that I had to carry my crown around everywhere I went. I had a box built to hold it, complete with purple velvet on the outside. But when I got spotted in the airports, people mobbed me, wanting to see the damn crown.

The worst thing about being the "King," however, was what the WWF wanted me to do as part of the gimmick. They wanted me to portray an effeminate king who ordered servants to do his bidding, and who complained that everything wasn't just perfect.

I refused. Harley Race may not be the most charismatic guy in the world, but I am who I am. I've never portrayed myself as anything other than who I am. Why would I let the WWF turn me into a laughing stock toward the end of my career?

They weren't happy when I told them that I wasn't about to act like this queer king character for some idiotic WWF storyline. So they made Bobby Heenan my manager, and had him do my talking for me, which suited me fine. Heenan would just say,

"The King doesn't feel like speaking today, so I'm here to speak for him."

During the late 1980s, I was spending quite a bit of time with the British Bulldogs. Dynamite, Davey Boy and I were on many of the same cards, and we would travel together most of the time. Some called the 1980s the "decade of greed," but it was also a decade of excess. In the WWF, that translated to "bigger is better."

Traditionally, wrestlers have always been pretty big guys. But in my era, you didn't have to have the look of a chiseled bodybuilder to be a superstar. Now things were changing. The WWF was giving big pushes to guys like Hulk Hogan and The Ultimate Warrior—guys who looked bigger than life not only in person, but also on television.

At the time, I was in my mid 40s. I had been one of the biggest stars the profession had ever seen, and now I found myself competing for top billing with guys half my age who looked like they pumped iron 20 hours a day. Dynamite and Davey Boy had the look, too. They weren't naturally big guys, but they were all muscle.

If I ever needed a boost to my physique, it was now. So one day I asked Dynamite and Davey Boy how they got that look to their bodies. I pretty much knew the answer before I asked the question. "Steroids," they simply said. Many of the guys had started taking them to bulk up. Dynamite told me that most of the guys got them from a doctor in Hershey, Pennsylvania. He encouraged me to give it a try, and—to tell you the truth—it didn't take much arm-twisting. I wanted to add muscle mass, and that seemed to be the answer.

There were many different types of steroids, but when I read the print on the bottle of mine, my mouth dropped open. A warning on the bottle said, "If you're going to eat the meat, do not inject the horse." This crap wasn't even meant for humans—it was for horses.

Halfway through a six-week cycle of steroids, I could already start to see the results. Dynamite told me that to get the most out of them, you needed to hit the weights pretty hard. Whatever hotel we stayed at, he and Davey Boy often could be found in the hotel's gym working out. I was never a big weight lifter, and previously I never needed to. God blessed me with a good amount of strength, and for much of my career I got all the conditioning I needed by wrestling hour-long matches each night. But now I was taking injections of anabolic steroids and working out in the gym on a daily basis with The British Bulldogs.

By the fourth week, I was clearly adding muscle to my body, but it came with a price: the pain in my lower back was intensifying. I asked Dynamite if the steroids caused him any pain, and he said they did. "It just goes with the territory, mate," he said. It didn't take an Einstein to figure out why: I was a 260-pound man taking steroids designed for a 2,000-pound horse.

By week five, the combination of steroids and weight training were giving my muscles a good pop. But the pain in my lower back was only getting worse.

"I've got enough pain," I thought to myself. "Why in God's name do I want to subject myself to even more damn pain when I got along fine without this steroid crap?" So I quit five weeks into the cycle, and I've never touched anything like them again. I didn't lose a whole lot of muscle when I quit simply because I hadn't taken them long enough to gain too much.

When it came to steroids, the difference between me and Dynamite was that I had been one of the top names in wrestling for more than 30 years without them. I didn't need them, even during the twilight of my career. Dynamite was an average-sized kid who used steroids and weight training to pack 240 pounds on a frame designed for 180 pounds. He knew that if he got off the juice, his body would deflate back to its original size and he'd be out of a job. Or at least he'd be knocked down to the midcard level. He was a hell of a talented wrestler, but he grew up in an era when size mattered. Like many of the guys, he did what it took to get big.

A couple years later a steroid scandal would give professional wrestling a black eye. But it wouldn't change things. Some of the guys said they weren't worried about their supply being cut off—they kept stockpiles in their refrigerators that would last several years.

Did I regret my decision to try steroids? I'd be lying if I said I didn't have mixed feelings. On one hand, I had the ability, I just needed the look to keep up with this new era of muscle-bound wrestlers. If I had kept taking them, I clearly would have regretted it. I can't say I regretted quitting them. A lot of young wrestlers think steroids are an instant shot at success, or the only shot they'll have. And for some, that's true. But what kind of trade-off are you willing to make for that shot at success?

The purpose of the King of the Ring tournament was to quickly elevate my status in the WWF up to the level of a champion, without mentioning that I was a former champ of another organization. Then they would pit me in a series of matches against their own world heavyweight champion: Hulk Hogan. One of those matches that would virtually force me into retirement.

I've already told you that the diving head-butt was the stupidest thing I've ever come up with. (Not that it wasn't a good effect—audiences loved it. But decades of performing the stunt contributed to a lifetime of serious back problems.)

Another stunt that I pioneered did as much damage in an instant as diving head-butts did through decades. I'm talking about being thrown through a table.

It's a great effect that's still used today. Perhaps the best-known instance of a wrestler going through a table was when The Undertaker tossed Mick "Mankind" Foley off the top of a 16-foot cage into a table during a 1998 "Hell in a Cell" match. It's considered one of the greatest matches of all time.

As far as I know, I'm the first wrestler to be thrown through a table. In hindsight, I realize that probably wasn't the quickest way to get my MENSA application approved. But there's no doubt it had a high entertainment value, and that's what I always strived for.

The first time it happened I was wrestling Pat O'Connor in St. Louis. I was pissed off at the state athletic commissioners because the bastards would ring the bell and end the match whenever someone would go off the top rope to do an aerial maneuver. So I told O'Connor, "Pat, hit me, I'm going to take out those timekeepers."

"No, no, no, you'll get us sued," he shot back.

"Just do it," I said.

You can't have much more of a conversation in the ring than that without people catching on, so, against his better judgment, he complied. I took the bump, spun around and flopped directly onto their table. The table's legs collapsed and the table fell to the floor, skinning the legs of a couple of the commissioners. Of course, I had a pretty good laugh at their expense. I also noticed that they never sat their table that close to the ring again. I thought I was pretty clever. But I should have known what goes around comes around—my newfound stunt would damn near kill me when I performed it on another occasion.

The next time I thought to try it was about a month before the matches with Hogan. I was wrestling Randy "Macho Man" Savage. I had Savage outside the ring on the announcers' table, and I told him: "When I go to the top and you see me leave the top rope, roll out of the way."

"All right, what are ya gonna do?!" Savage barked back in his gravely voice.

"Just roll off, I think I can go through it," I said.

I climbed to the top rope and Savage got out of the way just in time. As I crashed into the table, it imploded, sending particles shooting 15-20 feet outward from each of the four sides.

Word of the stunt got back to Vince, and he wanted to see me perform it against Hogan.

In March 1988, at least half a dozen matches were scheduled between Hogan and me in the cities including Los Angeles, Oakland, Boston, Baltimore, St. Louis and Kansas City and New York's Madison Square Garden. While the King of the Ring tournament was designed to build up my status to make me a viable challenger to Hogan, these matches were intended to make Hogan look like the unstoppable force he was through much of that decade. In each match, he either won or we wrestled to a draw. In some contests, he would win by a fluke. Like the match at Madison Square Garden, where I had him beat in the middle of the ring. I got out of the ring and took the WWF Heavyweight championship belt, placed it over his motionless body, then climbed to the top rope to fall head first into him. Only he moved the belt at the last moment, leaving me to dive into it. Hogan then covered me for the three-count.

Hogan's wins would put him in line to regain the title, which he held for four years straight until losing it to Andre the Giant in 1988. He would use that momentum to go on the following year to win the title for the second time, this time from Randy Savage.

It wasn't planned this way, but the night I did the table stunt with Hogan turned out to be the last in our series of matches. It's a crazy enough stunt as it is, but here I was in the twilight of my career, letting Hulk Hogan toss me through a perfectly good table. You'd think we would have used some sort of rigged table, like the breakaway bottles that actors always used in those old western movies. But "safety first" isn't exactly the motto of professional wrestling, so, of course, we didn't think of that. Like an idiot, I didn't even go out to the ring and look at the table before the match.

Like before, I had no problem going through the table when I hit it. It didn't even hurt that much. Until I tried to get up, that is. That's when the steel band that wraps around the edge of the table recoiled and hit me just above the pelvic bone. I would have been better off if the damn thing would have just hit the bone and broke it. Still, I just shrugged it off and kept wrestling. That's not to say that it didn't hurt. It burned like hell.

About a week later, I started feeling abdominal pains. But pain was nothing new. I had learned to live with a lot worse. So, again, I shrugged it off and kept going. I kept wrestling, and I was looking forward to Wrestlemania IV, just weeks away. It would be the first WWF tournament in which 14 wrestlers would compete for the heavyweight championship. In a WWF first, the title had been deemed "vacant" after Andre the Giant tried to give it to Ted DeBiase. I skipped the tournament, competing instead in a battle royal, which was won by Bad News Brown.

After Wrestlemania, I returned to Kansas City. At the time, I was living in an apartment with Justin. I was toward the end of a bitter divorce that dragged on through most of the 1980s and wasn't finalized until 1990. (Forgive me if I don't spill all the ugly details, but I've been trying for years to repress them, and it's finally starting to work.) Justin had left to go to a night class, and I tuned in to see an NCAA Final Four college basketball game. It was right about halftime when a horrendous cramp took hold of my stomach. The pain was strong enough that I lost consciousness and didn't come to until the game had ended. Now, I've learned to live with pain, but this wasn't ordinary pain. If you've ever had kidney stones or given birth, you might have an idea of the type of pain I'm talking about. It's the kind of pain that makes your mind think irrationally, "Maybe if I hack off my hand with this dull steak knife, then I won't notice the pain in my stomach so much."

So I called my doctor, who told me to get to the hospital ASAP. Shortly after arriving, I blacked out.

EIGHTEEN

DEATH'S DOORSTEP

"I saw the man when he could hardly walk. He would carry in a suitcase the world championship belt. His back was bothering him. He sat on the bench in the dressing room, found someone who would rub his back with their elbows. Then they'd tell him it was time to go out. He'd put his boots on, comb his hair, and for one hour he would tear down the house and take every kind of bump you could imagine. He was going through tables when guys couldn't spell 'table.' And he didn't go home after a match and have a glass of Ovaltine, he stayed out and had a good time."

—Bobby Heenan

I woke up a day later in the hospital, but I wasn't sure if I was alive. And I was in no condition to ask the doctor whether I was alive, and, if so, how long I would stay that way.

Apparently, I wasn't in any condition to empty my bowels on my own because there was a colostomy bag next to my bed.

I can make light of my predicament now. At the time, of course, no one was laughing. My intestine had inflamed and ruptured, and I had peritonitis, an inflammation of the membrane that lines the inside of the abdomen and all of the internal organs. That, in turn, had caused a deadly bacterial infection. I was too ill to understand what my doctor was telling me at the time, but if you cut through the medical jargon, he was basically saying, "Harley, you're pretty much screwed."

I wasn't told at the time, but it was basically a flip of a coin as to whether I would live or die. No kidding. Even if I knew how dire my condition was, it wouldn't have really mattered to me. I was in too much pain to care either way.

Well, to end the cliffhanger, I didn't die. But you knew that. Within 30 minutes of stumbling into the emergency room, the doctors were cutting open my stomach. They repaired my intestine, which had spewed feces and deadly bacteria into my body when it burst. Not a pretty picture. So they cleaned off my guts, sewed me up, and gave me some life-saving antibiotics. (Anyone who had what I had just a few decades earlier would have kissed his life goodbye. With antibiotics, deaths in these situations are much more uncommon.)

Surgeons performed a colostomy on me, and they told me I would need to wear a colostomy bag for a year. After three months, I went back and told them to take it off. "If I die, I die," I told my doc. "If I don't, then all the better. Either way, I'm rid of this thing."

After six months, I was itching to get back in the ring. I knew I was at the end of my career, but it's hard to give up something you've done your whole life. I didn't know anything else. A lot of people who can't wait to retire don't like their jobs to begin with. Well, despite the fact that I was past my prime and wrestling was destroying my body, I still pined for the sensation of rolling into the ring, holding a belt high above my head and hearing an auditorium roar to life with cheers, boos, cat calls, chants and insults. As long as they had a reaction, and as long as they kept coming, I knew I must have been doing something right. I loved the hookups and pins and everything in-between: the tackles, submission holds, knee drops and aerial maneuvers.

So instead of listening to my doctor's wishes, everyone around me, and my own body, I started wrestling again. But because my doctors wouldn't give me the OK, neither would the state athletic commissions. So I had to leave the country. At the time, Vince Jr. was making a push into Europe. He sent me to Paris, Italy and other places in Europe, where I alternated between wrestling Hogan and Andre the Giant. I wasn't at 100 percent, but I was able to wrestle.

Andre was in worse shape than I was. The physical punishment of wrestling couldn't hold a candle to the toll on his body from his Giantism disease. In fact, he had quit wrestling and returned to his native country of France until Vince convinced him to wrestle again in Wrestlemania III. He was depressed and basically waiting to die. When he did get back in the ring, his range of movement was even more impaired than usual. After a match, it hurt him just to walk. He suffered constant back pain, and his heart was having increasing difficulty pumping blood throughout his 500-pound body. But he rarely complained. Andre only had a few short years to live. He "retired" after Wrestlemania VI, but continued to wrestle off and on for All Japan Pro Wrestling through December 1992, often teaming with Baba. He died in his sleep on January 27, 1993, not long after attending his father's funeral.

I returned from Europe without aggravating my injury, but it wouldn't stay that way for long. Because of my stomach problems, my weight had fallen from 260 to under 200. Keep in mind, this was the time in the WWF when steroids were all the rage, and bigger was better. But I couldn't bulk up or keep the weight on. My stomach problems weren't going away, either.

Doctors cut into my abdomen several more times to clean out the dead tissue so that it would heal quicker.

By late 1988, it became apparent I needed to slow down. Vince offered me a job booking for the WWF, but I turned him down. I knew we had different philosophies about running the business, and I knew we'd be butting heads. That's when the WWF talked to me about passing my "King" title to another wrestler. I essentially needed to abandon my title because of my injuries.

One by one, the WWF named wrestlers who they would like to see the crown passed to—the Honky Tonk Man and Brutus the Barber Beefcake to name a couple. And one by one, I shot down the names. Maybe it was a point of stubborn pride, but Harley Race wasn't going to lose his final title to just anyone. It had to be someone I liked and respected more than most. Plus, I didn't want my successor to be someone who got the title because of politics. (Brown-nosing Hulk Hogan gained Honky and Brutus enough brownie points to be in contention.) I wanted someone who could defend the title in and out of the ring, if it came to that. Finally, the name Haku came up.

As a kid in Japan, he helped carry my bags when he was breaking into the business. We had been friends ever since, so I couldn't think of anyone more appropriate than to pass my title to. Incidentally, it would be the first time Haku would win the title "King," but it wouldn't be the first time he used it. In a previous incarnation, he was "King Tonga."

The match occurred at the Royal Rumble pay-per-view event on January 15, 1989. I knew that in all likelihood this would be the last time I held a title. So, in addition to my family, I flew C.B. and Martha Ball to Houston to watch it.

Don't feel bad that you've never heard of them. They're not famous. Years earlier, I was in a Kansas hospital with an infection, and C.B. Ball walked in my room to visit me. I had never seen or heard of the guy in my life. But it turned out he knew probably more about my career than I did.

C.B. was just a fan, but he was a smart one. He knew that visiting me in the hospital was the one way he could meet me. Plus, he sincerely cared about me and wanted to see how I was doing.

He and his wife, Martha, became family friends. It was a friendship that lasted two decades until he died well into his 90s. The guy was a genius. He played chess with people from around the world by mailing their moves back and forth. He often played chess with my son, Justin. So I thought it only fitting that my No. 1 fan and his wife got to see me on my last night as King Harley Race.

Stubborn me, I had been reluctant to give up my title at all. But I came to realize in this match that I should have done it sooner.

Because this was my swan song, and because I was passing the title to my friend Haku, I wanted to wrestle with the same intensity that garnered me international fame earlier in my career. So for one final time, I climbed to the top. The audience knew what was next, and their cheers rose to a crescendo. As I dove head first, Haku rolled out of the way and I landed hard on the canvas. I immediately felt my innards start to rip. (By this time, I was wearing a back brace that I turned around to protect my stomach. But I don't think the manufacturer meant for it to be used while performing a diving head-butt.) Haku finished me off with a thrust-kick, which was his finishing move back then.

The match with Haku would be my last match with the WWF.

I had reaggravated my abdominal injury, but the strain didn't seem that bad after the match. Still, I should have gone straight to the hospital. Instead, I went to Japan. I had already missed two other tours in Japan: once at Vince's request and once because of my injury. I didn't want to let them down for a third time, and I didn't want to risk not being asked back. Plus, my stomach hurt, but not bad enough to sideline me.

During my two-week tour of Japan, I toned down my risky moves in the ring. The first thing I did away with was the diving head-butt. No one wanted to see my guts spilled out onto the mat, especially me.

My abdominal pain wasn't too bad after the tour, but I knew I needed to get it checked out. At the University of Kansas

Medical Center, they performed the seventh and final abdominal surgery on me. They basically removed part of my innards and let the skin regenerate over my stomach. I had to change the wrappings on my stomach twice daily. To this day, my stomach is scarred and disfigured because of the injuries and operations. The injury also left me with a hernia between two scars in my stomach.

When I was trying to keep the NWA alive, I viewed Vince McMahan Jr. like small software companies view Microsoft. The WWF was the Evil Empire and Vince was its leader. But I have to give him credit—he treated me well in the WWF, and even paid me when I was laid up with my stomach injury. He didn't pay me what he would have had I wrestled, but, then again, he didn't have to pay me at all.

I spent the middle part of 1989 recovering. It was during that time I was approached for a business proposition. Several American businessmen wanted to try to sell dome-shaped manufactured homes to the government of Bolivia to use as public housing. They asked me to be their celebrity spokesman and offered to fly me first-class to Bolivia. The profit potential sounded nice, so I flew there and talked with several officials from the country. We even built one of the homes as a demonstration. Meanwhile, I saw Bolivia as a new market for professional wrestling, so I took some initial steps to try to bring a show into the country. To draw interest, I made a promotional tape of myself and other American wrestling stars. It featured not only wrestling clips, but promos of us talking about wrestling in Bolivia. Then I had it aired on Bolivian television.

In the end, neither of the ventures got off the ground. The Bolivian government told us they no longer needed our help, and then proceeded to do a similar project on their own. So they essentially stole our idea. I didn't do enough research on what it would take to bring wrestling into Bolivia, so that was a bust, too.

I didn't make any money, but I didn't lose any either. Nothing ventured, nothing gained, I figured.

Even before my match with Haku, Vince had talked about the possibility of me becoming a road agent for the WWF. The job essentially would consist of traveling with the wrestlers and making sure everything runs smoothly at the shows. Sort of like a theater production manager.

The problem was that I already had experience in every part of the wrestling business, and I had my own ideas of how things should be run. But this didn't seem to be a job that had room for my ideas. It seemed to be the kind of job that was by the book—the WWF book. I couldn't see myself reduced to saying, "yes, sir' and "no, sir" every day when I didn't agree with what I was doing. So I turned him down and considered my other options.

NINETEEN

MOVING INTO MANAGEMENT

"Every time Harley came through Texas, he'd ride with me. I wanted to be around him. I admired his work and his toughness. Another thing we have in common is a need for speed."

—Ted DiBiase

By 1990, the NWA had essentially folded. Jim Crockett then morphed the only remaining viable part of the NWA—Georgia Championship Wrestling—into World Championship Wrestling (WCW) in 1983. But between bad luck and bad management decisions, Crockett was forced to sell the company or fold, and he found a willing buyer in Ted Turner.

Turner reportedly called Vince after buying the company to boast: "I'm in the rasslin' business."

"That's fine because I'm in the entertainment business," Vince supposedly shot back before hanging up.

The two powerhouses were well into their battle by the time I joined the WCW in 1990. By this time, I was past the point of swearing any allegiance to one company or another. I just wanted to continue in the business I love, and hopefully continue my standard of living while doing it. Ole Anderson, who was booking for the WCW at the time, lured me to the organization. He offered me a contract that allowed me to manage other wrestlers full time while still wrestling in a limited capacity.

I wrestled right from the start, but my matches were few and far between. I had nothing more to prove in the ring, but I did have something to prove outside the ring. I wanted to show people that I had the ability to bring up young wrestlers and make them world champions like I was.

Dusty Rhodes called, offering me my first managing assignment, an up-and-coming wrestler named Larry Pfohl. He wrestled as Lex Luger, a knockoff name of Superman's archenemy, Lex Luther. Luger was six feet, five inches tall, and weighed 265 pounds of pure muscle. He looked like a Greek god.

Right around the same time, they put me with other wrestlers, including the Kolossal Kongs, The Super Invader, Yoshi Kwan, Vinnie Vegas, and Mr. Hughes. In most cases, I didn't really "manage" the wrestlers they put me with. I just showed up at ringside for their matches to give them a boost of credibility, especially if they were wrestling acts that were literally or figuratively bigger than they were. One exception was Steve Austin. I knew he had the potential to be a top act and told anyone who would listen. I think some of the others at the WCW, including Dusty, could also see his potential.

When Luger started gaining popularity, I wound up spending 90 percent of my time with him. Unfortunately, that left me with little time to spend with Austin or any of the others. As it turns out, of course, he did just fine for himself without my help.

The WCW wanted me to not only manage Luger, but mentor him as well. From the start, there was no doubt Luger had the tools for stardom. But there were a couple areas in which he needed help. One was with the microphone.

Now I've never been known as one of the best talkers in the wrestling industry, and I wouldn't want to be. I've always preferred to let my wrestling speak for itself. But as far as doing interviews and cutting promos, I think I've always held my own. And I've done it without having anyone put words in my mouth. Whatever you've heard me say has come out of my head, not out of a scriptwriter's pen.

Like many managers, I typically acted as Luger's spokesman and did most of the talking for him. When I was finished, he'd chime in with a little something to reinforce what I just said.

I also helped him out in the ring. As a heel (he had recently switched from babyface), he was supposed to be the ring general, controlling the flow of his matches from inside the ring like an orchestra conductor controls his musicians in the pit. Throughout my career, it was one of the things I did best, and something that made the name Harley Race what it is today.

Luger was able to get his matches off to a good start, but he didn't have the repertoire of moves to keep it flowing. So I would call him to ringside to suggest different offensive moves to use against his opponent. Sometimes when a match started falling flat, I'd have Luger throw his opponent out of the ring so I could take a couple of shots at the guy before tossing him back. In the business, when a manager picks on a guy's opponent—usually behind the referee's back—we call that "cheap heat." Getting Luger and his opponent out of the ring also would give me a chance to tell Luger what series of moves to do next.

As a manager, I went out to the ring with the same enthusiasm and goal that I did as a wrestler. My attitude was that when the WCW put me out there with Luger or anyone else, they would know I'd do what it took to get the match over with the fans.

I often drove Luger from match to match in the early '90s, and we sometimes spent the time talking about the mental part of wrestling: how to use different series of moves to put together a good match so it flows well in the ring. I gave him tips that hopefully helped him have great matches regardless of the skill level of his opponents.

While riding together, I would tell him what to do in certain situations and what combinations of moves worked best together. Then I'd quiz him later. He was no dumb jock—he had the ability to remember nearly everything I told him, and he was able to incorporate it in his matches. He was sometimes known for being stubborn and refusing to listen to advice, but I have to say that he really did want to learn from me, and I think he did.

July 1991 was Luger's big break. Flair had recently jumped to the WWF, and the WCW World Heavyweight Title was up for grabs. Luger defeated his old tag-team partner Barry Windham in a tournament to win the belt. He kept it for another seven months before losing it to his buddy Sting.

By this time, Luger's wrestling and his title had raised the eyebrows of higher-ups at the WWF, and he soon jumped at their offer to join. Vince Jr. saw Luger's strengths and weaknesses, and he eventually turned Luger to a babyface.

Luger's grand turn in the WWF was an open challenge on July 4, 1993, on the USS Intrepid, an aircraft carrier docked off the coast of New York City. It was the perfect way to switch his character from a hated heel to a patriotic babyface.

During the event, Yokozuna made an open challenge for anyone to body-slam him, and Luger was the man who did it. Luger never won the WWF championship belt, but he went on to have a stellar career that included returning to the WCW and winning the belt again, this time from Hogan.

After Luger left the WCW, that left me to mainly manage the one wrestler who had more natural ability than any of the others I've managed: Big Van Vader.

Leon White was an NFL standout who was a starting outside linebacker for the 1989 Super Bowl Los Angeles Rams. At six feet, five inches tall and weighing 456 pounds, he was as round as Luger was chiseled. Don't be fooled, though. He was the most agile big guy I've ever seen. In fact, he might be the best big man ever to enter the ring. Just don't tell him I said it.

Vader was decent with the microphone, and he could definitely hold his own in the ring. That wasn't the problem. The problem was getting him to hold back. While Luger wasn't naturally aggressive in the ring, Vader was a monster. He portrayed his football player/brawler image well—probably too well. Put it this way: He wasn't well-known for taking care of his opponents in the ring.

Once, Vader was hammering on Flair like a madman during a match between the two. I was managing Vader at ringside, and I could tell Flair was exasperated. Finally, I said, "Ricky, if you don't return those shots just as hard, he's not going to respect you, and you can expect to put up with that all night." So Flair popped Vader hard in the face, giving him a black eye. Vader behaved himself the rest of the match.

Another time, Leon nearly "vaderbombed" a kid into oblivion. The vaderbomb—his version of the powerbomb—was his finishing move. Well, it finished the match, all right. The poor kid was temporarily paralyzed. After the match, he went to visit the guy in the hospital and apologized up and down. Vader even cried for about an hour over the deal. After a few days, the kid finally got feeling back in his spine and neck.

Of course, the new "sensitive" Vader lasted for a couple hours, tops. Vader was the kind of guy who, if he didn't think you were of his caliber in the ring, he'd just run roughshod over you. The problem with that is that you quickly run out of people who will wrestle you. And if I told him once, I told him a jillion times, "Leon, lighten up or you're not going to have anyone to work with."

Usually, he'd just say, "Yeah, I understand what you're saying, Harley." But occasionally, he'd be more defiant and stubborn. "Hell with it," he'd say. "If they can't take it, they can get out of the business."

I believe it was during one of these conversations in a hotel room in Raleigh, North Carolina, that our conversation actually turned physical. We had been enjoying a few ice-cold foamy adult beverages when Vader decided he didn't like my constructive criticism. Soon enough, we were rolling around the floor in a brawl that was half serious and half fun. Together, we were 700 pounds of flesh rolling around in the living room area of the hotel. Of course, tables, chairs and everything else in the way were getting steamrolled in the process.

Did we worry about the hotel manager banging on our door? Nope. The manager, a friend of Flair's, was already in our room drinking with us. He's the one who broke us apart by screaming at us. The next day we were all on good terms again, but he billed us for the damage: $600 each.

While I was with Vader, he won the WCW championship twice in 1992 and once in 1993. In 1995, he got into a backstage brawl with Paul Orndorff, a great wrestler who was working as a talent agent for the WCW at the time. From what I heard, Leon pretty much got his ass handed to him on a plate during that fight. To make matters worse, the WCW canned him over it. To this day, Leon blames me for getting fired. An accident had forced me into retirement. (More on that later.) So Leon reasoned that if I had still been there as his manager, they would have spared him the axe. So for him, the logical jump in reason is that I was to blame for him getting in the fight and getting fired.

Leon was fine when he was sober or when he wasn't in the ring, but when he was either drunk or wrestling, he was your typical bully. That was his downfall. Fortunately for him, he's remained in the business, wrestling in Japan and, more recently, becoming an ultimate fighter for Pride. Shoot-style fighting sounds perfect for him; I don't know why he didn't do it sooner.

When I wasn't managing Vader or Luger, I was sometimes golfing with them. Sting also liked playing, so he often rounded out the foursome. At times, I was going to manage Luger or Vader against Sting that same night and we'd all be out earlier that day hitting the links. That wouldn't have happened during the days of the NWA territories. But by the early '90s, Vince Jr. had acknowledged in court that professional wrestling matches were predetermined, so there wasn't as much pressure for opposing wrestlers not to be seen together.

It was a smart move on Vince's part from the standpoint that it saved him a lot of money. By acknowledging that pro wrestling was more entertainment than sport, he eliminated oversight from many athletic commissions—and the taxes that went with it.

But many of the old-time wrestlers, including me, weren't happy with his admission. It seemed like a move to benefit him at the expense of the entire industry. But I can't say it was a surprise. It had been an issue that had been debated inside the industry for years, and I think it was a matter of time before it happened. Still, many of us old-timers were mad as hell.

Kayfabe was a code of secrecy that we took very seriously. To a certain extent, we still do. To this day, I tell my students that even though many people know that professional matches are predetermined, they shouldn't be smartening people up to the business any more than they already are. I also tell my students what we were told when I was a kid: "Don't be seen out socializing with your opponent. People want to suspend disbelief, just like when they go to the movies. Don't do anything to ruin that."

If people know they're predetermined, fine. But that doesn't make our business "fake." Not only does the term "fake" do our business an injustice, it's just plain wrong. The techniques, the innovations and, especially the pain, are all very real.

TWENTY

OUT OF ONE
RING, INTO
ANOTHER

"We were on an airplane once to Miami to take a cruise. While loading stuff in the overhead compartment, Dad saw these two, little-bitty straw hats, owned by these two ladies. Dad's sitting behind them, and leans forward so they can hear him, and says: 'I wonder whose straw hats I just crushed?' The ladies were squirming around for the next hour waiting to check their hats. Of course, the hats were fine."
—Justin Race

The 1990s ushered in a new era in my life. In the last chapter I told you how, at the age of 47, I had entered new frontiers in my career, while returning home to an old employer. Now, in this chapter, you'll learn what was happening in my personal life during that same time period. It was filled with ups and downs, but the highlight was that I was about to meet the woman who would warm my jaded heart and turn this gruff wrestler into a romantic.

Away from the ring, I'm more of an even-tempered and quiet man than you might imagine. But the year 1990 would test those traits through a roller-coaster ride of highs and lows in the span of just one year.

Well, what you have to realize is that during the first half of my career, I was spending money as fast as I made it. That's how I owned various cars, boats, motorcycles, even houses. Sure, I was a millionaire once I started saving. But divorce took care of that. In fact, it left me damn near broke. It was a dark time in my life, but even darker days were on the horizon.

By 1990, my divorce was final—it was a drawn-out process that seemed like an eternity—and I was once again a single man at the age of 47. One silver lining came out of all my legal woes: I had made friends with a couple of attorneys who had helped me, and they introduced me to a lady friend of theirs named B.J.

She was a vice president of Commerce Bank in Kansas City, and she seemed like a wonderful lady. "Perfect, I thought. I'll go out with her." The only problem was that when I asked her out, I got shot down in flames. I wasn't used to hearing "no" from anyone once, much less a year, but that's how long it took to get a date with her.

Meanwhile, Rob, B.J.'s son from her previous marriage, was putting in a good word for me. "Mom, you're not going to go out with him?" he would ask. "Do you know who that is? That's Harley Race!"

To which she responded: "Who's Harley Race?"

Not only was she intelligent and pleasant to be around, but she had never heard my name. That's part of what attracted me to her. Even after she found out that I was Harley Race, world-champion wrestler, she still wasn't impressed. So when I finally got a date with her, I knew it was on my own merits as a gentleman. She just got to know me well enough socially to trust me, and she gave me a chance.

Our first date was a simple lunch date, but I thought it went well. That is, until I asked her if she'd be willing to meet me at a restaurant for dinner. "This week isn't good," she said. I knew by her terse response that something was wrong. So I asked her, and she set me straight: "Where I was brought up, the man picks up the woman for the date." Ooops. She was right. I blew it. But fortunately, she gave me another chance after I asked her if I could pick her up for dinner. That was the only break I needed. I showed up with a dozen long-stemmed roses and a bottle of Dom Perignon. She probably appreciated the roses more than the champagne, since she had never heard of Dom Perignon. But she asked me, "What should I do with this? Do you want to open it right now?" I said: "Keep it in your refrigerator, and if I'm lucky enough to get another date with you, we'll drink it then."

It wasn't long before we fell in love.

Meanwhile, my wrestling career was coming to an end. By 1992, my wrestling matches were few and far between. And by 1993, because of accumulated injuries, I was pretty much resigned to working outside the ring, managing Vader. I probably wrestled a dozen times between passing the "King" title to Haku and my final match in 1993.

The match, held in Florida, was the main match of the evening. It was scheduled to be Vader vs. Flair. Only Vader missed his plane, so they polled the audience: Who would you like to see wrestle Flair tonight? By an overwhelming majority, they picked yours truly.

I knew I was getting old and far from the best shape of my life. But I never let the audience down before, and I wasn't about to let them down for what I knew probably would be the last match of my career. It was a championship match—scheduled to go for an hour—and Flair's title was on the line. So I grabbed the microphone and told the fans: "I don't know if I can go an hour, but I know that Ric Flair can't beat me in 30 minutes." So we set the time limit to a half-hour.

Behind the scenes, WCW officials scrambled to plan out the match. They asked me: "What would you like to do?" and "What are you willing to do?" Of course, what they meant was: "Are you willing to let Flair pin you?"

"I ain't getting' beat," I said. "The only two options are put-ting the belt on me, or we go the time limit."

That's what we did. We wrestled to a draw, and Flair kept his belt. It was the last time I entered the squared circle as a com-petitor, but it wouldn't be the last time I got into the ring to train or, for that matter, to entertain.

The feeling of knowing it was my last match was overwhelm-ing. I knew it was time to step down and time to concentrate on other parts of the business. But if I ever told you I didn't miss it, I'd be lying. Until the day I die, I'll miss that nightly hour in the spotlight. I'll miss the creativity and quick thinking it takes to put together an exciting match. I'll miss the crazy bumps—not just dishing them out, but taking them as well. I'll miss the other wrestlers. And most of all, I'll miss entertaining the fans.

It wasn't the end of the world. With my managing career, I was still in the game. I continued managing Vader, which was an enjoyable challenge. I wasn't wrestling, but I got to live vicarious-ly through him in a sense. But that, too, would be cut short in yet another life-threatening accident.

In January 1995, B.J. was out of town on a banking conven-tion and I went downtown to a bar to shoot pool with a couple friends—at least I thought they were at the time.

We started playing for fun, but one of the guys suggested we make it interesting and play for a little money. By the end of the night, I was down about $1,300 and physically feeling worse for the wear than the few drinks I had. Only later, after I started piecing things together in my mind did I suspect that I was the victim of a scam. My two "friends" were working as partners, and I was their mark. To make matters worse, I still suspect someone might have slipped something in my drink that night.

When I left the bar, I was driving across an inner-city bridge and ran across a pothole from hell that popped the airbag and jerked the car to the left. It was at an intersection where one concrete divider stopped at the start of the intersection and another one began at the end of it. I lost control of my car, and it plowed into the front of the barrier.

The impact pushed the engine block into the front seats, nearly crushing my legs. My right forearm and hip were both fractured. Doctors told me later that most people wouldn't have survived the wreck. I managed to get out of my car and stand up, but that was about it. I don't remember much after that.

It took a steel plate and four screws to put my hip back together. But my luck was about to go from bad to worse. Two weeks after the wreck, I developed gout in one of my feet. It's a build-up of uric acid that can cause intense pain and, if not treated, serious tissue damage. On this particular morning, I wasn't able to put any weight on my foot. I was in no shape to walk to my physical rehab class, and I told my nurse as much. Still, she insisted, and she got an aide to help lift me out of my bed. In doing so, they dropped me and I collapsed backward into a chair. I banged my head, but my body absorbed much of the shock. It was enough to fracture my hip all over again, this time in various places. You would think that would get me out of my physical therapy class for the day, but it didn't. At the time, they didn't know I had refractured my hip, so they insisted I attend the session. Why I complied I'll never know. It was pure torture, but I completed their bullshit exercises. Only after that, when they got me back to my room, did they perform an X-ray and determine that I had refractured my hip.

By this time, B.J. and I had dated exclusively for several years, and I had recently asked her to become my wife. She'll tell you that behind this gruff exterior there's a soft, cuddly teddy bear of a man. It's a side of me that only she's seen. (And if it's okay with you, dear readers, let's keep it that way.) But she'll also tell you that the way I proposed was about as romantic as being on the receiving end of a stink-face from Rikishi Phatu. In a supermarket parking lot, I took out a ring, and said, "Here, you probably already know you're getting this." We had already talked about marriage, so it was pretty much a forgone conclusion at that point. In retrospect, I guess a nice restaurant would have been a bit classier. (Plus, I should have had the foresight to realize how many people would say: "Ohhh, he proposed! How sweet. How did he do it?") Despite my lapse in romance at this crucial time, she still accepted my proposal.

At the end of December 1995, we invited John and Pat Edwards, couple friends of ours, to spend the weekend with us in southern Missouri near Branson. Their plan was to enjoy a relaxing weekend with fishing, boating and antiquing. Our plan was to share our day with our unsuspecting friends, who would also be the witnesses we needed to make it official.

After driving around for a while, Pat began to get anxious. "Why aren't we stopping at some of these antique shops?" she asked.

It was only after we pulled up to the Little Bells Chapel in Harrison, Arkansas, when they started to clue in.

"We don't know what you guys are going to do this weekend, but we're going to get married," I announced. I asked if they would be our witnesses, and we could see their eyes welling up with tears.

We caught them by complete surprise, and they were honored to be part of our special day.

The county's recorder of deeds even opened up his office on a Saturday so we could get our license. We had hoped to make it a small, private affair, but someone—it almost had to be the preacher—tipped off an area newspaper, which covered the event. I was surprised to see someone from the media there, but once they were, we went ahead and gave them what they needed for a story.

We got married on December 28, 1995, then had a wonderful honeymoon at southern Missouri's Lake Taneycomo, known throughout the Midwest for its great rainbow trout fishing.

Somewhere I must have walked under a broken ladder or stepped on a crack in the sidewalk, because I had just finished a seven-year period of bad luck awful enough to make the national president of the Optimist Club put a bullet in his head. As the band Cream once sang: "If it wasn't for bad luck, I wouldn't have no luck at all."

Through thick and thin, B.J.'s commitment to me never wavered. I'm afraid to think about what would have become of me without her.

I had shredded my insides by jumping through a table, then went through seven surgeries and God only knows how much pain to repair the damage. I had gone through a divorce that left me bitter and damn near penniless. I suffered through a horrible car wreck that left me with an artificial hip. But my marriage to B.J. was not only a ray of sunshine in an otherwise dark time in my life—it was a turning point.

TWENTY-ONE

REBUILDING YEARS

"Wrestling Harley was good for one simple reason. Harley was a villain a lot of times, but the difference was that Harley was a wrestler. He didn't go in there kicking and gouging people's eyes or hitting below the belt. Harley went in there and demonstrated his wrestling skills. He always wrestled, and he always provided what was right for the sport. I did my damnedest to bring respect to the business through my behavior. I've never heard of Harley doing anything that was a detriment to the business, in or out of the ring."

—Bruno Sammartino

E arlier in 1995 before I got married, I was wondering if even all the king's horses and all the king's men could put Harley together again. My injuries were piling up like cordwood. As a result of my fall in the hospital, fixing me this time would require another surgery. By going under the knife this time, I went from having one metal plate and four screws in my hip to two plates and 14 screws.

The WCW gave me six months' pay and released me from my contract. It was with the understanding that, if and when I was ready, my job would be waiting for me. But it never happened. Managing Luger and Vader was my swan song—it was my last full-time job with a major wrestling organization. Recuperating from my January 1995 wreck took between 12 and 18 months, and I never returned to WCW. Still, the organization treated me fairly, and I have no complaints.

Throughout 1995, my hip came out of its socket three different times. Each time, I had to be taken to the hospital by ambulance. When I left, I wore a brace from my hip down my leg. I wore that brace 24/7 for months, except when I showered. I was still wearing it on my wedding day.

When I wasn't going through physical therapy during 1995 and the first half of 1996, I was sitting on my ass watching TV. Specifically, I watched the O.J. Simpson trial—not just a little bit here and there, though. I watched the whole damn thing, from beginning to end. I was hooked on The Juice like women watch their soaps. And when the prosecution let O.J. try on the gloves, I just about lost it. That was the funniest part of the whole surreal affair. How could they be such idiots? It was a no-win proposition for the PA. Of course, the glove didn't fit, and they had to acquit. But in my opinion, O.J. was guilty as charged; that was a no-brainer.

Many of the guys called to check up on me from time to time, and it meant a lot. When I rehabilitated enough to walk, B.J. took me to Atlanta to one of her banking conventions. There I caught up with Luger and Sting and we shot a round of golf one afternoon. Well, I was barely in any condition to walk, much less play golf. So it must have looked pretty amusing to see a 260-pound guy swinging the club like a cripple, cringing in pain, and then watching my ball roll a few yards in front of my feet. In fact, the foursome behind us seemed to be having a good laugh at my expense, until Luger—all 6'5" and 265 pounds of him—approached them. "You damn sure have just better told a joke, because otherwise I might get the impression that you're laughing at my friend," he growled. They quickly apologized.

In 1997, despondent over injuries from my '95 car wreck, I put a gun in my mouth and pulled the trigger, ending my life. Before that, I succumbed to cancer. And before that, I died in that car wreck. You'll find various causes of my death on the Internet, but you shouldn't always believe what you read. It's like Mark Twain once said, "Rumors of my death have been greatly exaggerated."

I suppose the Internet is a great thing. But the computer generation isn't my generation, and I can't say I'm computer savvy. Hell, I can't say I could find the "on" button. But computers and the Internet have revolutionized our society, making information on practically anything easily accessible. Of course, the accuracy of that information isn't always guaranteed …

By spring of 1996, I was well enough to be up and about, but in no shape to continue the only career I've ever known. I had watched more TV in the past year than I had previously in my entire life. I needed something to get me out of the house. Something to keep me busy. Something to challenge me.

One day a couple of lawyers we knew mentioned that sheriff's deputies couldn't track down several people to serve them court summonses. Someone suggested: "I bet Harley could track them down." To me, that sounded like a pretty exciting challenge. So that brief conversation led to my next career: I became a court-appointed process server.

I know what you're thinking: How far of a fall must that be going from being "the best wrestler on God's green earth" to serving court summonses to losers who practically go in hiding so they don't have to pay their child support or alimony?

No, the gig didn't exactly stand up to body-slamming Andre the Giant in front of tens of thousands of screaming fans. But, then again, it was better than lying half-dead in some hospital, where the highlight of my day was getting my colostomy bag changed.

I took the job more for the challenge than the money. And it was a challenge. Plus, it was a part-time job that let me work when I wanted. Most of the people I served summonses to lived in the Kansas City area and had bad debt of some type. And many of them couldn't be located by sheriff's deputies to be served.

On a number of occasions, I was able to serve people because of who I am. One guy who lived in a high-rise building was able to avoid authorities because the building had a security officer. If you lived there, the officer called you to see if you wanted to let the person in to see you. All he had to do was say "no." But when I paid him a visit and said who I was, he replied: "*The* Harley Race?" "Yep, what's left of him," I replied. Of course, he came right down, and I served him.

Another guy lived in a dense wooded area near a lake and had avoided service because nobody else wanted to venture out in the boonies to find him. There was no answer when I knocked, so I hid nearby until I saw a light come on. When I served him, he voiced his displeasure by threatening to kick the shit out of me. "My friend, that's entirely up to you," I said. "But if you make the mistake and decide to try it, I'll guarantee you that you'll be the one who gets the shit kicked out of him." He wisely chose not to try.

One guy decided to sic his watchdog on me. The dog was foaming at the mouth when it charged me. When it got close enough, I pointed at the dog and screamed "sit!" The dog, apparently reflecting the idiocy of its owner, did as it was told. I slapped the dog's snout to put a little fear in him, then simply sidestepped the mutt. I jerked open the guy's front door just enough to throw the set of papers at him.

A couple times my encounters did turn physical. Once, I went to a guy's workplace for the third time in an attempt to track him down. The eight-month time period to serve him was just about to expire. If I didn't serve him this time, the courts would have to refile the paperwork on the guy. I was determined to not let that happen. So, with the help of his employer, I found the guy and threw the court summons onto his lap while he was trying to drive away in his car. When someone physically touches the papers, they're legally served. As you could imagine, the guy was angry as hell. He stopped his car, got out and threw a punch at me. I've blocked a hell of a lot stronger and faster punches in my life, and I wasn't about to let this one connect. So I deflected it, and then slapped the shit out of the bastard. As a process server, you do all you can to refrain from using force. But as far as I was concerned, this was self-defense. In any other situation, I would have done a lot more than just bitch-slap the guy.

Seeing the different reactions was the fun part of the job. They ranged from perplexed looks from people who said: "Harley Race? What are you doing here?" to fans wanting me to stay and chat. Some got their court papers and an autograph all at once. That's a full-service process server.

All in all, I served around 500 people between 1996 and 1999, and I'm proud to say I had a 100 percent success rate: There wasn't a single person I wasn't able to track down.

During this period in the mid- to late 1990s, I also passed the time by becoming the household's official maid and chef all rolled into one. Not only did I clean and vacuum, but I even occasionally mopped the floors. I didn't dust. A guy's gotta draw the line somewhere. Plus, I went on strike during football season.

But on most days, B.J. came home from her banking job to a clean home and a hot meal on the table. I enjoy cooking a wide range of dishes, especially one-skillet meals like cabbage and hamburger casseroles.

Another thing that helped me keep my sanity during the 1990s was the barbecue parties that B.J. and I threw for the guys when they came to Kansas City for wrestling events. Our parties started in the early '90s when I invited over half a dozen guys to B.J.'s Kansas City home one day. After getting razzed by the guys who didn't get invites, we decided to throw a bigger bash the next time the WCW came into town. From there, it turned into a regular thing, to the point where the guys didn't wait for invitations when they came to Kansas City. Instead, they'd just call and say: "What time should we be there?"

When Luger switched from the WCW to the WWF in 1993, he asked me: "Which guys at the WWF should I tell to come over when we come to town?"

"Just tell them all," I told them. We even had the ring crews, announcers and referees over.

Within a year or two, our parties evolved from intimate gatherings to parties with dozens of the top wrestlers in the country. Even the *Kansas City Star* wrote about a Thanksgiving feast we provided the wrestlers one year. It wasn't uncommon for us to drop close to $1,000 on food for each get-together.

Guys who typically came by included: Stone Cold Steve Austin, Kane, The Undertaker, Paul Bearer, Lex Luger, Ric Flair and The Rock.

A typical scene would be Buff Bagwell, Dustin Rhodes and Eric Watts playing cards in the living room, while Stone Cold would be crashed out napping on the couch. Some of the guys would be in another room watching tapes of some of my classic matches, while Big Van Vader would be apologizing for breaking another chair that he sat in. I could often be found outside manning the barbecue grill.

Kansas City is known nationwide for its top-notch barbecue. The next time you catch a Kansas City Chiefs game on TV, just wait until they pan the cameras to the parking-lot tailgaters. You'll almost be able to smell the tangy barbecue right through your TV set. So when I have people over for barbecue, I try not to disappoint.

B.J. constructed a huge, almost industrial-sized grill on wheels that works great as a smoker. I would start out by marinating ribs overnight the night before using a recipe that includes Italian dressing and a six-pack of beer. The carbonation in the beer breaks down the meat enough that it can better absorb the marinade. Then I would rub a mix of spices into the meat before tossing them on the grill and cranking it up to about 600 degrees. I let the temperature slowly cool off while the meat cooks over a period of a few hours.

Meanwhile, B.J. would make about two dozen different desserts. Combine that with potato salad, baked beans, home-made rolls and some foamy beverages, and you've got yourself a meal.

The guys were always appreciative and respectful. By the time they left, the trash was taken out, the dishes were washed and you could hardly tell anyone had been there. Of course, they could be a little ornery at times when they all got together. Once, Too Cold Scorpio hid several desserts in the microwave that he wanted to eat later. Steve Austin happened to see him hide the food, so he sneaked into the kitchen and ate every dessert, then put the empty plates back in the microwave.

Paul "The Big Show" Wight once asked for some dessert to take with him back to the hotel, and B.J. ended up giving him one of each. He left with sacks containing more than 20 desserts—enough to give most guys diabetes on the spot.

The guys would come over before the show to eat barbecue ribs and relax before their matches. Then they'd come back afterwards to have a few drinks and, during the winter, eat my home-made chili. The guys would unwind by bellying up to the bar and do shots from B.J.'s shot glass collection.

One time, Owen Hart was helping himself to a bowl of chili when he saw that Mick Foley was on his way over for the same thing. So Owen quickly dumped some Insanity hot sauce in the ladle after filling his bowl. The only problem was that Mick stirred the chili before taking some. So he essentially spiked the entire batch with hot sauce. Everyone's mouths were on fire that night, and Owen had a good laugh at our expense.

But in this business, payback can be a bitch. I got Owen back the next night when the guys were wrestling in Topeka, Kansas.

After his match, Owen walked out of the shower blissfully unaware of what I had prepared for him. I had a stun gun, and I pressed it right on his bare ass, giving him a good zap. All the guys were waiting and watching, and burst into laughter when they saw him get zapped. It took him a couple minutes to get his senses back, but all he could do was smile and shake his head—he knew he had it coming.

Owen was a special guy. I knew him and Bret since they were young boys. They were almost like younger brothers to me. I'll never forget the day Owen died—it was one of the saddest days of my life, and one of the saddest days for professional wrestling.

It was May 23, 1999, and I was attending a WWF Over the Edge pay-per-view event in Kansas City's Kemper Arena. Before the show, I was talking with Triple H and a few of the guys, when Owen walked by. I hadn't seen him in a long time. He seemed nervous, and he told us he was uncomfortable with a stunt that he was being asked to perform. His Blue Blazer character was to be lowered from the rafters into the ring by a cable.

"I'm really afraid of it," he said.

"If you're afraid of it, don't do it," I advised him.

But I think he felt obligated to go forward with it, and that it was too late to back out anyhow.

As he headed out that dressing room, I uttered a prophetic wisecrack: "Be careful that rope doesn't break," I told him. If only I would have known.

B.J. hugged him and asked if he felt any better.

"The only thing that makes me feel better is your cooking," he said before heading off down the hall.

I was standing backstage watching the monitor when the lights dimmed. Before Owen started his descent, a quick-release mechanism was triggered as Owen was adjusting himself while dangling in a harness. He plunged 78 feet into the ring ropes, landing lifeless in the ring. It was a sickening feeling watching him fall, and I knew the odds of surviving such a fall would be slim.

Emergency personnel converged on him quickly, and people began screaming for an ambulance. Meanwhile, many of the fans didn't initially realize that what they saw was real. They cheered, thinking that a mannequin had been dropped. For a few seconds, they thought it was just another wrestling stunt taken to the extreme for shock value.

When they put Owen in the ambulance, I saw Sgt. Slaughter conferring with the first responders. From a distance, I pointed my thumb up then down, then shrugged my shoulders. He pointed his thumb down.

I followed the ambulance to the hospital. Less than 30 minutes later, a doctor came into the waiting room and gave me the news I was dreading: They were unable to revive him. Owen was dead.

The doctor asked if I had contact information for his family. I told him that I did, and that it might be best if I made the call. I called his parents and broke the news to his father, Stu, who I knew very well. Both had watched the incident on television. They were awaiting word on Owen's condition, hoping for the best, yet expecting the worst.

After I got off the phone, Jeff Jarrett ran into the ER waiting room, and I told him that Owen had died. He called WWF brass at Kemper Arena to break the bad news. The WWF made the snap decision to continue the show.[1]

I've been asked dozens of times what I think about that decision. I've always said the same thing: It might sound cold-hearted to some people, but I think they made the right call. When tragedies strike in other sports—auto racing and football, for instance—they go on with the show.

Good decision or bad decision, we had still lost a good friend. The next time the WCW came to town, Bret Hart wrestled Chris Benoit in a tribute match to Owen. At Bret's invitation, I announced the match and spoke a few words in Owen's memory beforehand. It was tough to talk to the fans that night, and I could imagine it was even tougher for Bret to wrestle in the same arena that his brother recently died in.

---

[1] *Broken Harts: The Life and Death of Owen Hart* contributed some information on the account of Owen Hart's death.

TWENTY-TWO

BRIEF RETIREMENT

"When Harley came to Eldon, there were some people who took a wait-and-see approach. The way profession-al wrestling is under Vince McMahon doesn't exactly reflect a good family image. But it didn't take long for everyone to realize that Harley runs a show you can bring your grandmother to and not be embarrassed. He's a good friend and a Masonic brother."
—Kyle Mason, former Eldon city administrator

"I'm going to retire," B.J. announced one evening as we sat down to eat dinner in June 1999. "Life is too short—we should enjoy whatever time we have left on this earth, and do what we want."

Although my wife's announcement was out of the blue, it was hardly unexpected. Six members of her family had recently died, the last of which were her sister and brother. Plus, Owen Hart had recently died in the ring. The deaths hit both of us hard, and forced us take a strong look at our own mortality.

We decided to move to the lakefront vacation home at Lake of the Ozarks, which we had bought in 1995. Within a week, we had our Kansas City home on the market, and by August we were both officially retired at the lake.

By September, we needed something to do.

It wasn't that we weren't enjoying retirement, but we were already starting to get an itch to do something. Or at least I was. I had been working a part-time job as a process server that left me plenty of time during the past three years to cook, clean and watch more than my share of bad TV. I had worked in the wrestling business since I was 15, often seven days a week. Going from that to a part-time job outside of the business was fine at the time, but it wasn't wrestling.

The only thing I had ever known was the wrestling business. I had started in this business as a young teenager with nothing more than desire and the God-given ability to make my dream come true. I worked my way to the top, and I worked with other rising stars and got to see them go all the way as well. What I hadn't done was use the lifetime of knowledge that I had acquired to help kids make it in this business. Lots of college-aged kids have that same desire and ability I did, but finding a place to learn pro wrestling isn't as easy as signing up for a class at your local business college.

When I was starting out, several people went out of their way to give me a chance and teach me about wrestling, including guys like Ray Gordon, Bobby Graham and "Killer" Buddy Austin. So did the Zbyszco brothers, who, despite the fact that one was in his 60s and the other in his 70s, kicked the shit out of me on almost a daily basis and called it "wrestling training." Still, they all gave back to their profession by helping a young punk like me. Maybe it was my turn to give a few eager kids a chance they wouldn't otherwise have.

It was with that thought that I decided to start my own wrestling school. Fortunately, I was able to convince B.J. to come out of her two-month retirement to help me start the business. I knew all about wrestling, but when you throw around terms like accounting, spreadsheets, inventory and taxes, my eyes start to glaze over. But B.J., with her 30 years of banking experience, knows about all that and more.

We picked Eldon, Missouri, to start our operation. Eldon, population 5,000, is located between Lake of the Ozarks and Jefferson City, the state capital. This Mid-Missouri town is best known as one of the filming locations for the 1960s television show *Petticoat Junction*. We found a building for rent right smack in the middle of the city's downtown. It was the perfect location at a reasonable price, so we bought the business and took over the lease on the building. We sectioned it off with a wall, leaving half of the space for the Nautilus equipment, tanning beds and bathrooms and the other half for the wrestling ring and offices for me and B.J. It was nothing fancy, but it did the trick.

We continued to operate the gym, while advertising for recruits for the wrestling school, which I named the Harley Race Wrestling Academy. The first class featured about a half-dozen students who eagerly plopped down $3,000 each for a course that, on average, lasts six months. Fast learners might graduate in half that time, while others take longer than the average. From the start, my plan was to get them to learn what they needed to wrestle professionally, however long that took.

The kids all had varying degrees of talent. Most of them thought they had wrestling experience, but it was mostly variations of "backyard wrestling"—crazy stunts that involve lots of danger and little wrestling. It would have been better if they'd had no experience at all.

I hired Derrick "The Sheik" Stone to be my head trainer. He had two or three years' experience on the independent wrestling scene. Derrick had good technique and was a good teacher. He was the one who spent the majority of time in the ring with the students, while I often critiqued their performances from ringside. Occasionally I would jump into the ring myself when I felt the need to show a certain move or technique.

Not long after I started, I had a cocky student who decided he was going to teach me a thing or two about wrestling. We were on the floor beside the ring. I was teaching the group of kids about the hookup—the first contact wrestlers have with each other at the start of the match.

When I went to hook up with the kid, he pulled a fast one on me. He sidestepped me and performed a sweep, an amateur wrestling move in which he used my own momentum to sweep me onto the ground and quickly get on top of me.

He was a young kid with a background in amateur wrestling, and he was in pretty darn good shape. I was in my mid-50s, out of shape and had a handicap sign in my vehicle because of injuries accumulated from a lifetime of taking bumps. It wasn't a fair match—but I wasn't about to tell the punk he was in above his head. He needed to learn a little respect.

Once he got on top of me, he proceeded to taunt me in front of my students. "So this is Harley Race, the best wrestler on God's green earth?"

By this time, the group of students fell silent. Like a train wreck, it was painful to watch, but they couldn't avert their eyes.

"What are you gonna do now, champ?

"You're just an old man," he said. "I'm gonna pin the eight-time world champ."

He continued to show off in front of the other kids, telling me what accolades he won as an amateur high school wrestler. When he seemed to be done showboating, I asked him: "Are you done, kid?"

"Why? What are you going to do?" he sneered.

Without answering, I faked a roll to one direction, and when he tried to counter the move by throwing his weight in the other direction, I rolled in the opposite direction. I gave him a taste of his own medicine by using his own momentum against him. Immediately after the roll, I caught him in a cross-face—a painful submission move that I had used off and on throughout my entire career.

A second later, he was literally screaming, to the delight of everyone watching. "Who did you call an old man?" I asked.

When I eased up on the hold enough for him to breath a little, he changed his tone. "You're the king, Harley, you're the king! Please, let go!"

I later took him back to my office to have a chat with him. "The dumbest thing you ever did was come into my backyard and try to show me you knew more about wrestling than I do," I said. I told him he was welcome to stay in the school, but that he needed to adjust his attitude. "You're here to learn, not teach," I told him.

He ended up leaving the school not too long after that. I remember him saying that he thought professional wrestling would be easier—not harder—than amateur wrestling.

Many of the kids who have entered my school have no idea what it takes to wrestle professionally. Even the ones who say they've had some wrestling training typically know as much about wrestling as a grade-school kid who turns on *Smackdown* on Thursday nights. First, it's physically demanding—something I teach them from Day One. The cardio workout I give each student on his or her first day lasts just 30-45 minutes, but it's excruciating. Most of them, even the ones who were standout high school wrestlers, wind up puking their guts out by the end of that first workout.

I've never done this to try to "break" them like you hear about in the Marines. I'm not trying to weed out the weak from the strong so much as I'm giving them a gut check, and showing them that this profession isn't about posing for the cameras and signing autographs. Unless you get into it for the wrestling, and unless you put your heart into it, there's not going to be anyone to stick a camera or a pen and paper in your face.

From the start, my kids all learned at different rates. But I never gave up on any of them. I'm not the kind of coach or instructor who gets in your face and yells if you don't remember something or do it right, even if it takes several tries. That tactic wouldn't have worked on me, and I'm not going to try it on these kids. Patience is one thing I learned as a coach involved in amateur wrestling when my son was in grade school. You can't teach wrestling to young kids like that and not have patience.

Pro wrestling can be even tougher to teach. Learning how to do things that your body isn't designed to do takes time and commitment. It's not natural to have your body hoisted six feet in the air and slammed onto your back. And even when you land the right way, it's gonna hurt. Land the wrong way, and you'll get injured. Land the wrong way constantly, and your body won't make it to retirement age. Ric Flair is one of the few guys I've seen who can land wrong on a consistent basis. Ever since breaking his back in an airplane crash in 1975, he's avoided landing flat on his back. It started out to protect his weakened back when he returned to wrestling, and it became a habit that he does to this day. I guess it's not landing wrong if it works, but I wouldn't advise this to anyone else.

Not only have I let my students learn at their own pace, but I've also encouraged them to develop their own style. "I don't want you to be a young Harley Race," I tell them. "You need to develop an identity of your own."

I tell them that the most important thing they need in wrestling is stamina to go through a match without "blowing up" halfway through—meaning running out of steam. The second most important thing is to have an imagination. By that I mean the ability to think up and execute different combinations on the fly. It's OK to try to learn the moves done by your favorite pros, but don't stop there. Add your own twist to the move. That way, you're not just stealing someone else's moves, you're putting your own stamp on them by taking them to a new level.

TWENTY-THREE

TEACHING A NEW GENERATION

"I know how the business is and how dishonorable peo-
ple can be to make sure they get ahead. I can call
Harley and say this is what I need. I don't have to have
anything on paper or doubt whether this is what he's
going to do. I love coming up here and working for
him, because I love everything he's about."
—Ron Harris

S oon after I started the school, the media caught wind of it.
The *Jefferson City News Tribune, Kansas City Star, St. Louis*
Post-Dispatch, Columbia Daily Tribune, Springfield News-
Leader and the Associated Press all came to my new school to
write stories about it. And that was just some of the print media.
Radio and TV came, also. The media coverage gave my fledgling
business a boost in several ways. Not only were more students
coming, but the public was interested to see what these kids
could do.

Shortly after opening the wrestling school, I started a wrestling league to operate in conjunction with the school—World League Wrestling (WLW). It was only natural that by training the kids, they needed an outlet to perform. So through WLW, I started booking events throughout Missouri and sometimes in neighboring states.

People ask me what I think about the state of the wrestling industry these days. I can sum up my thoughts of the direction pro wrestling has taken with the motto I picked to represent WLW: "Shut up and wrestle." At the risk of sounding like the old-timer who tells his grandkids about how he walked 10 miles through snow to get to school each day, here's how I feel: The wrestling industry used to be, first and foremost, about wrestling. All the posing, flexing, fan interaction and promos took a back seat to what happened in the ring. Not anymore. Now, the storyline is the event, and the wrestling is often a five- 10-minute sideshow. And the storylines themselves are constantly pushing the envelope. It's not enough to have two women wrestle each other, now they've got to rip each other's clothes off. Instead of just being a patriotic wrestler, now you have to be a bigot who espouses his hate for Mexicans. I guess the big-wigs at the WWE know what draws viewers, but I'd like to believe there are enough fans of pure wrestling out there to keep the ratings high.

I've tried to make my WLW shows a return to wrestling as I know it: less talking, more wrestling. I try to keep my shows clean of profanity so people can bring their families. And I try to keep them affordable: usually $10 for general admission tickets and $15 for ringside seats.

A typical event works like this: charity organizations interested in sponsoring an event call our office. If they're a decent organization and have the manpower to promote the event (and if the event is in a town that can draw several hundred people) we'll book it. The charity group finds a location—often a high school gymnasium or armory—and promotes the event through the media and by putting up flyers throughout the city. In turn, the charity group gets a percentage of the gross profits.

Our job is generally to coordinate details with the charity groups and then put on the events. As far as the wrestlers on the cards, it's a combination of my kids from the school and wrestlers I bring in from other areas. Each card typically has a combination of singles and tag-team matches as well as women's matches and midget matches. For the main event, I usually fly in a big name. That's the single most expensive cost of an event, but it's needed to get a good turnout. And a good turnout isn't just good for the benefit organization and me; it's also good for my kids to gain experience wrestling in front of bigger audiences. I'm still friends with many of the top wrestlers, and a number of them have been kind enough to wrestle for my organization. Among others, I've brought in Rick Steiner, Buff Bagwell, Meng, Dustin Rhodes, Diamond Dallas Page, Abdullah the Butcher, the Disco Inferno and Ricky Steamboat. Even Mick Foley guest refereed a match in spring 2004 for me.

Our events are classic slices of Americana. We often hold them in high school gyms in smaller towns. During intermissions, I'll go into the ring to introduce special guests. In one recent show, we honored a young man from Eldon who just returned from serving in Iraq in Operation Iraqi Freedom. He just returned home in August 2004, not long after the United States turned over the government in Iraq to its people.

Typically, I'll also take time to tell people in the audience that if they want to learn wrestling, learn from a professional school. That backyard-style wrestling will get you paralyzed or killed a lot quicker than it will make you famous. In other words: "Don't try this at home."

From the start, I told my wrestlers that the issue of whether to take steroids is a personal decision. It's a decision I tell them they'll have to make on their own—that is unless they're training at my school. "As long as you're here, don't take them. Period," I tell them. "That goes for illicit drugs, too. When you leave my school, you can make your own decisions. But as long as you're here, it's forbidden."

When I started this business in 1999, there were probably a couple dozen independent wrestling organizations in the Show-Me State. As I write this, there are only a few others left besides mine. To tell you the truth, most independent wrestling organizations aren't real big moneymakers. The only reason ours has survived is because of who I am and the knowledge I brought into it. Like many businesses, it took ours a couple years before it went from operating in the red to operating in the black. But I will continue to operate it with the same enthusiasm that I had whether I wrestled for a few thousand dollars a year or $400,000 a year. You have to understand that in my business plan, money is second and wrestling is first. It's always been that way, and it will be that way until the day I die.

Lately, it seems like wrestling has kept me busier than ever, even though I don't mix it up in the ring anymore. In 2004 alone, I've written this book, put on a wrestling camp, done dozens of interviews with media throughout the world, and had another back surgery (This one resulted in several ounces of metal being removed from my back.) In 2004, I was inducted into the WWE Hall of Fame and Pro Wrestling Hall of Fame and Museum. (I previously was inducted into the WCW Hall of Fame.) I've also participated in a WWE storyline that had "Legend Killer" Randy Orton spit in my face leading up to him winning the World Heavyweight Championship belt in August. I got scores of e-mails after that, criticizing Vince Jr. and the WWE for what my fans viewed as tasteless stunt. But I've been friends with Orton's father and grandfather, and I did it to give the kid a boost. In reality, Randy Orton has always been a gentleman and nothing but respectful to me, and I count him as a friend, also. So no, I don't regret it.

All that is in addition to running my wrestling academy and putting on wrestling shows most weekends.

The city officials and townspeople in Eldon have been wonderful. They've bent over backward to make my wife and I feel at home here, and we've made many new friends throughout town. Since moving here, I truly feel like a part of the community. I've held wrestling matches here to raise money for the city's high school booster club, fire department, little league, downtown merchants, chamber of commerce and Noble Eagles. We've earned around $60,000 for various charities and not-for-profits, just in the Eldon community alone. I've gone boating with the city administrator. I've even become a member of the local Masonic Lodge.

At lunchtime each day, when I walk across the street to eat my blackened grouper sandwich (one of the best grilled fish sandwiches you'll ever taste), the people in Buzzer McGee's restaurant/sports bar know me. They mostly all know each other, too. It's sort of like Cheers.

In 2001, Noah, a startup wrestling company in Japan, asked me to be their U.S. talent agent. It's been a mutually beneficial relationship. I've sent several of my graduates on tours in Japan, as well as several guys who have worked in the WWE or WCW, such as The Harris Brothers. Some of my former students realized, like I did back in the 1960s, that wrestling is huge in Japan, and they can make good money by touring there often.

On July 10, 2004, Noah flew me to Japan to attend the organization's first match at the Tokyo Dome. It was B.J.'s second trip to Japan, and – I believe – my 71st. In the few short years of its existence, Noah has become a contender for the top wrestling organization in Japan. Their match at the Tokyo Dome sold more than 50,000 tickets, and featured one of the best wrestling matches I've seen in my lifetime. And I've seen my fair share of matches.

They introduced me at one point in the match, and I could hear a throng of thousands begin to chant: "Hawlee Lace! Hawlee Lace!" The mispronunciation may sound funny to most Americans—the Japanese have always had trouble pronouncing r's, replacing them instead with l's—but it was endearing to this old wrestler. It's hard not to get emotional when you can travel halfway around the globe and have that many people still care about you enough to chant your name.

I was also honored when Mitsuharu Misawa, who formerly wrestled as "Tiger Mask II" and now is Noah's president, said that some of the greatest moments of his career were while he was in the ring with me. "Harley's achievements in pro wrestling have made him a legend," Misawa said in a recent interview. "All the wrestling fans in Japan recognize him as the NWA champion."

Joe Higuchi, a wrestler who also refereed more than 20,000 matches in 32 years before joining Noah's board of directors, also had kind words to say recently: "I have the utmost trust in Harley not as just a pro wrestler, but more importantly as a person. He is the kind of person who can understand other people's pain and feelings. Believe it or not, this is very important as a professional wrestler. Harley has a magic quality to get along with people, and he was able to adapt to Japanese culture very well."

Misawa, Higuchi, Ken Hirayama and everyone at Noah all have my utmost respect. It's a pleasure working for a wrestling organization with such honor and integrity.

Some of the young wrestlers I started training in '99 are still working for me five years later. And a couple of them travel to Japan on a regular basis to wrestle for Noah. None of my students have reached superstar status yet, but I've taught at least a couple who have the potential. When the WWE holds matches in the area, they often call me to see if I have any guys who could fill a slot for dark matches, the warm-up matches held before they turn on the TV cameras. It's a good way to give the guys a chance to be seen by a large crowd and the WWE. At the same time, it gives the WWE a chance to showcase new people during preliminary matches, and at relatively little expense to them.

So what advice would I give today's generation of wrestlers? After you get your body in shape, get your mind in shape. Because two of the most important things you can have in professional wrestling are creativity and an imagination. Don't try to memorize sequences or routines for your matches. Get comfortable enough in the ring that you can improvise.

And one piece of financial advice: Save and invest your money wisely while your career is on the upswing. Because no matter how famous you think you are, your earnings will go downhill as sure as your body will.

Young wrestlers are so eager just to perform and be in the limelight, that they don't care if they're making $25 a show. Unfortunately, the average wrestler isn't the guy with a $10-million contract from WWE. The average guy is someone who slugs it out on the independent scene, just trying to make a living wage.

Wrestlers have always been their own No. 1 enemies because they haven't banded together to watch out for themselves. I know the word "union" is a bad word for some people, but wrestlers would be smart if they organized in some fashion that would at least give them health insurance and a pension.

After I had my car wreck in 1960, when I was just breaking into the business, the original Sheik, Eddie Farhat, sent me a check for $25 a month for nearly a year while I recuperated. The guy barely knew me—we had wrestled each other once. By the time I was in a position to repay him, he wouldn't take a nickel back. It's an act of generosity I never forgot. I remained in touch with him over the years until he died in 2003.

Not everyone's been as fortunate as me. I've seen the industry chew up and spit out way too many wrestlers, who find themselves financially and physically broke later in their lives. Performers who risk their own health for people's entertainment deserve better.

After moving to Lake of the Ozarks and starting my operation in Eldon, it dawned on me that I've come full circle in more ways than one.

I'm now working in the same small town that I once wrestled in while climbing my way up the ladder in the early 1970s.

I started out as a simple country boy in a town where people wave as they drive by, even if they don't know you. I've ended up in a similar rural Missouri town—the kind of town where you slow down, rather than speed up, at a yellow light. In between the two towns, I've given my all to be the best at what I do. I lost enough sweat to fill an Olympic-size swimming pool, and shed enough blood on the job to make slaughterhouse workers cringe. Through the grace of God and a lot of hard work, I made it to the top of my profession—not once but eight different times.

Along the way I've gone through several lifetimes worth of physical and emotional pain. But the price I've paid has been a small one to live such a charmed life. People sometimes ask if I'd do it all over again, and to me it seems like such a no-brainer. Of course I would. And if I did it a second time around, there's not a whole lot I would change in my personal life, and even fewer things in my professional life.

When it's my turn to go to the great squared circle in the sky, I hope I leave a legacy as not only being one of the best at what I did, but I also hope I'm remembered as someone who taught another generation of wrestlers what it takes to be "the best wrestler on God's green earth."